The World's
GREATEST CRIMES OF PASSION

The World's
GREATEST CRIMES OF PASSION

Tim Healey

HAMLYN

First published in 1990
by the Hamlyn Publishing Group
Reprinted 1990, 1992, 1993

This edition published in 1997
by Chancellor Press,
an imprint of
Reed International Books Limited
Michelin House, 81 Fulham Road
London SW3 6RB

ISBN 1 85152 868 7

Printed in Great Britain by Cox & Wyman, Berkshire

Contents

Acknowledgements

A book of this nature must inevitably draw on existing published material. The author wishes to acknowledge his particular debt to:

Crimes of Passion, Treasure Press, 1983; *Strange Crimes of Passion*, Leonard Gribble, John Long, 1970; *A Crime of Passion*, Stanley Loomis, Hodder and Stoughton, 1968; *Crime of Passion*, Derrick Goodman, Elek Books, 1958 *The Chalkpit Murder*, Edgar Lustgarten, Hart-Davis, 1974; *'Orrible Murder*, Leonard De Vries, Macdonald and Jane's, 1974; *Vintage Murder of the Twenties*, Gerald Sparrow, Arthur Barker, 1972; *Crime and Detection*, Julian Symons, Studio Vista, 1966; *Forty Years of Murder*, Professor Keith Simpson, Harrap, 1978; *Murder: 'Whatdunit'*, J.H.H. Gaute and Robin Odell, Harrap, 1982; *Tragedy in Three Voices*, Sir Michael Havers, Peter Shankland and Anthony Barrett, Kimber, 1980; *The Minister and the Choir Singer*, William M. Kunstler, Gollancz, 1964; *Society Sensations!* Horace Wyndham, Robert Hale, 1938; *The Trial of Ley and Smith*, Ed. C.E. Bechhofer, Roberts, Jarrolds, 1947; *The Trial of Rattenbury and Stoner*, Ed. F. Tennyson Jesse, William Hodge, 1935; *The Lives of the Gallant Ladies*, Abbé de Brantôme, (trs. Alec Brown), Elek Books, 1961; *A Pictorial History of the Wild West*, James D. Horan and Paul Sann, Spring Books, 1954; *Murder and its Motives*, F. Tennyson Jesse, Harrap, 1952; *A Book of Trials*, Sir Travers Humphreys, Heinemann, 1953; *Lord Darling's Famous Cases*, Dudley Barker, Hutchinson, 1936; *The Sex War and Others*, Rayner Heppenstall, Peter Owen, 1973; *Young Thomas Hardy*, Robert Gittings, Heinemann, 1975; *Royal Murder*, Marc Alexander, Muller, 1978; *English Treason Trials*, C.G.L. Du Cann, Muller, 1964; *Crimes and Cases of 1933*, Roland Wild, Rich & Cowan, 1934; *The Trial of Bywaters and Thompson*, Ed. Filson Young, William Hodge, 1923; *The Burning of Evelyn Foster*, Jonathan Goodman, David and Charles, 1977; *Encyclopaedia of Modern Murder*, Colin Wilson and Donald Seaman, Arthur Barker, 1983; *Detection Stranger than Fiction*, Leo Grex, Robert Hale, 1977; *Mrs Harris*, Diana Trilling, Hamish Hamilton, 1982; *White Mischief*, James Fox, Jonathan Cape, 1982; *The Trials of Mr Justice Avory*, Bernard O'Donnell, Rich and Cowan, 1935; *Ten Real Murder Mysteries*, Sidney Sutherland, Putnam, 1929; *Doctors on Trial*, Michael Hardwick, Herbert Jenkins, 1961; *Doctors of Murder*, Simon Dewes, John Long, 1962; *Ruth Ellis, A Case of Diminished Responsibility?* Laurence Marks and Tony Van Den Bergh, Macdonald and Jane's, 1977; *Crime Within the Square Mile*, Ernest Nicholls, John Long, 1935; *Twelve Against the Law*, Edward D. Radin, Heinemann, 1950.

The publishers wish to thank the following for their kind permission to reproduce the pictures used in this book:
Topham Picture Library 15, 16, 18, 35, 38, 41, 47, 48, 51, 59, 71, 76, 105, 108, 112/3, 113, 115, 117, 135, 138, 143, 146, 166, 175, 179; Mary Evans Picture Library 21, 64, 81; National Portrait Gallery 62; BBC Hulton Picture Library 88/9, 89, 120, 123, 144, 155, 165, 166/7.

Introduction

Love, jealousy, revenge and despair – they are themes which everyone can understand. It may be hard to grasp the psychology of the mass murderer or the sex killer. But you do not need to be a monster to sympathise with the injured mistress in the bar-room saga of Frankie and Johnny:

> She shot her man
> 'Cos he was doin' her wrong.

This is a book of love stories in which someone feels themselves to be wronged – and someone pays the price. Often, the drama that unfolds will involve three people, figures caught in the eternal triangle which has wrecked loves and lives since the dawn of time.

In France and in certain other Latin countries, a special leniency is reserved for those charged with the *crime passionnel*. Broadly speaking, the term covers any crime due to lovers' jealousy or despair. If an outraged husband, for example, shoots his wife's lover he may secure a complete acquittal. The assailant is seen as defending the sanctity of his marriage, and the law is prepared to be flexible.

No such system operates in the Anglo-Saxon courts. The term 'crime of passion' is popularly used to describe any kind of offence rooted in the frenzies and frustrations of love. Jealousy, of course, remains the recurrent theme in real life as in folklore and literature. The 'green-eyed monster' lurks behind the majesty of Shakespeare's *Othello* as it does behind the honky-tonk chords of *Frankie and Johnny*.

A wealth of cases are described in the pages which follow: high romances, mysteries and horror stories – as well as some purely ludicrous episodes. What unites all the crimes is their passionate nature. Even the most coolly accomplished were conceived in the turmoil of hot blood.

Chapter
One

Hell hath no fury

Playwright William Congreve is credited with the words, 'Hell hath no fury like a woman scorned.' Actually what the dramatist wrote was,

Heaven has no rage like love to hatred turned,
Nor Hell a fury like a woman scorned.

Either way, the truth is the same. And when a proud woman is rejected by husband or lover social status counts for little. Pauline Dubuisson was a medical student; Ruth Ellis a night club manageress; Yvonne Chevallier wife to a government minister. All succumbed to the same driving passion to destroy the man she had loved.

'I'll Kill Him!'

When 23-year-old Kittie Byron stabbed her lover to death on the steps of a London post office, the charge really had to be murder. And murder in 1902 was a hanging offence. It made no difference that Arthur Reginald Baker had behaved like a brute towards her; no difference that, when the flood of her fury was spent, she collapsed sobbing on his crumpled body, calling pitifully: 'Reggie . . . Dear Reggie . . . Let me kiss my Reggie . . .'

The crime was committed in broad daylight before a dozen witnesses. She had stabbed him twice: once through the back and once through the breast. The second blow was probably the one that killed him. He died almost instantly.

Yet everyone's sympathy was with the frail, dark-haired girl who had wielded the knife. The coroner's jury, for example, brought in a verdict of manslaughter. The officials were incredulous, and the coroner himself asked: 'Do you mean unlawful killing without malice?'

'Yes,' insisted the foreman, 'killing on the impulse of the moment. We do not believe she went there with the intention of killing him.'

In fact, all the evidence suggested that Kittie Byron went there with precisely that intention. And when she was brought for trial the following month, it was on a charge of murder.

For some months before the fatal episode, Kittie Byron had been living with Arthur Reginald Baker in rooms at 18 Duke Street, off Oxford Street, in the West End. Baker was a married man and a member of the Stock Exchange. But that did not prevent him from presenting himself and his mistress to the landlady as 'Mr and Mrs Baker'. He drank heavily, often knocked Kittie about, and on one occasion half strangled her. But Kittie was loyal. She never touched liquor herself, and tried to shield her lover from the consequences of his actions.

Events came to a head on the night of Friday 7 November 1902, when the landlady heard a furious row erupt in the bed-sitting room. She went up and entered; bed-clothes had been thrown all about and lay in chaos on the floor; to one corner was a hat which had been ripped into shreds. The landlady confronted the drunken Baker, but Kittie interceded. 'Oh, there's nothing the matter,' she said, 'We've been playing milliner.'

Not long after the landlady left the room, the quarrel broke out again. It went on all evening, and at 01.15 the householder went back again to try and stop it. She found Kittie in the corridor, shivering in her nightdress. She was plainly terrified – yet still she insisted that nothing was the matter.

The next morning the landlady gave the couple notice to leave the premises.

A weekend of calm followed, and on Monday morning Baker even took Kittie a cup of tea before leaving for the office. She kissed him goodbye – a domestic scene – nothing hinted at the coming drama. The date was 10 November 1902, the day of the fatal stabbing.

The whole sequence of events emerged clearly at the trial. Just before he left the house, Baker asked the landlady for a private word. He requested that they be allowed to stay in the house after all. The landlady, however, insisted that they must leave. It was then that Baker informed her that Kittie was not his wife. The girl was the cause of the trouble, he said. She was 'no class' and would leave tomorrow.

The conversation was overheard by a housemaid who immediately told Kittie that Baker was going to cast her aside. 'Will he?' fumed the enraged girl. 'I'll kill him before the day is out!' She made her own preparations for going out, and confessed to the landlady about the phoney marriage. 'Then why don't you leave him?' asked the landlady, who had assumed that only wedlock kept the couple together. 'I can't,' said Kittie, 'because I love him so.'

She went to a shop in Oxford Street and asked a cutler for a long, sharp knife. He showed her a large item with a sprung blade that fitted into the hasp. She seemed too slight a girl to handle it, and the cutler suggested alternatives. No, said Kittie, she had a strong grip, and she proved it by operating the spring action several times. Having bought the knife she slipped it into her muff and made her way to a post office in Lombard Street. The building stood in the heart of the City where Baker worked. It was Lord Mayor's Day. The crowds were out in the streets.

From the post office, Kittie sent Baker an express letter bearing the words: 'Dear Reg. Want you immediate importantly, Kittie.' But the messenger boy could not reach Baker at the Stock Exchange and returned to Lombard Street with the note. Kittie insisted that he go back again. The boy did so – and this time located Baker who returned with him to the post office.

Staff at the post office had noticed the girl's excited state. And they also noticed an absurdly trivial dispute which arose when Baker arrived. An extra charge of two pence had to be paid for the messenger boy's time. Baker flatly refused to hand the sum over; Kittie insisted that it be paid and offered her lover a florin. Somehow, the incident speaks volumes about the relative characters of the couple. Baker was still refusing to pay as he left the post office, with Kittie rushing after him. The staff noticed something flash in her hand as she made her exit.

She caught him on the steps. The two blows were swift, and bystanders noticed no blood. In fact, the several witnesses at first thought she was striking him with her muff. Baker may well have been dead before a workman grabbed Kittie's hand and the knife fell with a clatter to the pavement. The trance of her fury was shattered, and it was then that Kittie fell sobbing on her lover's body: 'Let me kiss my Reggie . . . Let me kiss my husband . . .'

Kittie Byron made two different statements to the police shortly after her arrest. In the first she said: 'I killed him wilfully, and he deserved it, and the sooner I am killed the better.' In the second: 'I bought the knife to hit him; I didn't know I was killing him.' At the trial which followed she only managed to whisper: 'Not Guilty' as her plea to the indictment.

She made a pitiable figure in the dock, a pale and delicate girl whose dark eyes wandered dazedly around the court. She wore a blue serge suit and a shirt whose white linen collar was high about her throat, fastened with a black tie. The court heard that her real name was Emma Byron, but it was not hard to see why she had earned the diminutive of 'Kittie'. Sir Travers Humphreys, then a junior brief for her defence, later recalled how she clung to the wardress who brought her into the dock: 'It seemed as if she would break down at the very outset.'

Some twenty witnesses were called by the prosecution, and Kittie did break down. It happened as a surgeon was indicating on his own body the position of her lover's stab wounds. A stifled wail was heard. All eyes turned to the dock where Kittie was racked with violent sobs.

The defence called no witnesses – not even Kittie herself. Her counsel was Henry ('Harry') Dickens, son of the great Victorian novelist, and a man who had inherited his father's genius for stirring the emotions. Dickens tried to make out a case for Kittie having intended to commit suicide rather than murder. It was an improbable thesis which ran contrary to the evidence. He was on safer ground in pointing to the plight and character of the injured girl, and in touching the hearts of the jurors.

The judge, in his summing-up, was candid about his own emotions: 'Gentlemen of the jury, if I had consulted my own feelings I should probably have stopped this case at the outset.' But he was equally candid in dismissing manslaughter as an appropriate verdict. The jury was out for ten minutes. They found her guilty of murder – but with a strong recommendation for mercy.

The form had to be observed. The black cap was brought forth, and the dread sentence was passed. Kittie, weakly professing herself innocent of wilful murder, was to hang by the neck until dead.

But she never did. Great waves of public sympathy had gone out to the frail and mistreated girl. A huge petition was quickly raised asking for a reprieve and no fewer than 15,000 signatures were obtained in a single morning. Three thousand signatures were raised from among the clerks at the Stock Exchange itself. In the event, the petition was never formally presented to the authorities, for the Home Secretary granted the reprieve before receiving the document.

Kittie Byron's sentence was commuted to penal servitude for life. In 1907, her sentence was reduced, and she was released the following year.

Death of a Minister

Pierre Chevallier's public career had been a story of brilliant success. He came from a family of well-to-do doctors and served as a medical officer during the early months of World War Two. As a result of his bravery in tending wounded soldiers under fire he was decorated. When the Germans occupied his native city of Orléans, Chevallier continued to practise medicine by day, but by night he headed the local Resistance. Before the Allies arrived to liberate the city, Pierre Chevallier had bravely led the attack which drove the Germans out.

Elected mayor of Orléans at the age of only 30, Chevallier threw himself into the task of postwar rebuilding. So masterfully did he manage the work that Orléans was officially cited as the best reconstructed city in France. Chevallier became parliamentary representative for Orléans. And on 11 August 1951, he won an even greater honour. Aged 41, he was given ministerial rank in the new government of René Pleven.

The following day, Pierre Chevallier returned from Paris to Orléans as Under Secretary of State for Technical Education. He was driven down in a big, black limousine decorated with the official tricolor cockade. He only really came for a change of clothes – there were ceremonies to attend. His wife Yvonne was waiting at their home, and told their younger son Mathieu to run and greet him with the words, *'Bonjour, Monsieur le Ministre'* (Good day, Minister).

The child ran to the doorway with his greeting. Chevallier was delighted with the reception, and tenderly hugged his son. There were, however, no joyous greetings for his wife.

Chevallier went upstairs to change clothes in the bedroom. Yvonne followed him up. There was a quarrel – and she shot him four times with a 7.65 mm Mab automatic.

Downstairs, little Mathieu heard the shots and started crying. Yvonne went down to comfort him and hand him for care to a maid. Then she returned to the bedroom. A fifth shot was heard – and a fifth bullet drilled into her husband's corpse.

He had been a minister for precisely one day. Soon, the whole of France was to learn that behind the glittering façade of Pierre Chevallier's life lay a story of failure – the failure of a marriage.

Pierre and Yvonne had married before the war. She was a nurse of peasant background who worshipped the dynamic young doctor. From the outset, Pierre's family considered the marriage a mistake, never really accepting it. And

13

their judgement seemed to be confirmed as Pierre's fortunes rose. Yvonne lacked the social graces, becoming tongue-tied at dinners and receptions. When the smart talk started she would fall silent. A dull girl, his colleagues would say afterwards, a bit of a liability.

In fact, she loved her husband passionately, and none of her failings need have mattered if Pierre had returned her affection. But he did not. Bit by bit, Yvonne became distanced from her husband's career and concerns. The abyss opened when one of their two sons grew ill. The child's little bed was brought into the couple's bedroom while the sickness lasted. Pierre took to sleeping in his study. And when the boy recovered, Pierre continued to sleep in his own room. He never returned to the marriage bed.

The seed of suspicion was planted in Yvonne's mind. One day, searching through his pockets, she found a love letter to Pierre signed by someone called 'Jeanette'. She strongly suspected that it was written by a mutual friend, Jeanne Perreau, who was 15 years younger than herself. After a clumsy attempt to get a sample of her handwriting, Yvonne went round and accused her rival to her face. Jeanne denied that a liaison existed and back at home, Pierre told his wife to shut up and mind her own business.

But the suspicion did not die. Jeanne Perreau was the wife of a wealthy department store owner. She was a beautiful woman with luxuriant red hair and a very opulent figure. Above all, she was witty and sophisticated, shining at precisely those functions which for Yvonne were an ordeal. In June 1951, Pierre won his parliamentary seat and gave a lavish reception. His wife saw him there flirting openly with Jeanne Perreau. Yet when Yvonne herself tried to embrace her husband, he rebuffed her in front of everybody.

There was a terrible row that night. Yvonne demanded an explanation; she begged Pierre to return to their marriage bed. He replied cruelly that not only did he not want to make love to her – he did not even think himself capable of it. She had disgraced him at the reception: 'Can you really see yourself at the big banquets in Paris?' he taunted.

Pierre said that he wanted a divorce. Failing that she should take a lover. Yvonne was outraged and refused to countenance a separation. She loved him far too much for that.

Tensions were building up now to the point where something had to give. Yvonne had, for some time, been taking drugs: tranquillisers to make sleep possible, stimulants to nerve her for the day. She drank coffee in great quantities and smoked incessantly. And it was in this state of dangerous disorientation that she took the children off for a seaside holiday. From the coast she wrote a passionate letter to her husband saying that she would try to improve herself as a wife. Pierre did not reply. And when she came back, Yvonne took poison in an attempt to end her life.

Jeanne Perreau in the witness box

THE WORLD'S GREATEST CRIMES OF PASSION

Yvonne Chevallier

She only just failed, and was desperately ill afterwards. Every attempt to get through to her husband met with cold scorn on his part. Yvonne followed Pierre to Paris and tried to see him at the Chamber of Deputies. She was told, through an official, that he was too busy. Then she ransacked his flat in the city, seeking evidence of his betrayal. She found it in the form of a railway timetable. He had ticked off the times for Châtelguyon trains – Jeanne Perreau was holidaying there.

Yvonne returned in a rage to Orléans and confronted the husband of her rival. M. Perreau at first tried to soothe her fears. But after a second visit he admitted that he knew Jeanne was having an affair with Pierre. Léon Perreau was not the least distressed about it either; he was one of those curious characters beloved in French farce – a *mari complaisant* or compliant husband who simply did not mind being cuckolded.

But Yvonne was no compliant wife. Pierre had found out about her trip to Paris and phoned her to call her a 'cow' and tell her to stop ruining his life. It was after this call, and Perreau's admission, that Yvonne went out and obtained a firearms licence.

There was no problem in getting the certificate; her husband was now an important political figure and she claimed he had dangerous enemies. Armed with the certificate, Yvonne went to a gun-shop where she asked for a weapon that was guaranteed to kill. They sold her the Mab automatic.

Killing was clearly in her mind – but killing whom? On 11 August Yvonne heard over the radio that Pierre had been appointed a minister. Immediately, she sent a warm telegram of congratulation. Then she contacted a nun who was a close friend and told her that she was going to commit suicide.

The nun, of course, advised her against the act. Pierre phoned later from Paris saying that he would be coming back the next day to pick up some clothes. He did not thank her for the telegram. Perhaps it was his curt and disdainful manner that mingled thoughts of murder with those of suicide.

She spent a terrible night. The next morning, Pierre's name was blazoned across every newspaper. Chevallier a Minister! – no mention, as customarily, of the loving wife. That must have rankled. Still, she mustered up enthusiasm to get little Mathieu to say his party piece – 'Bonjour, Monsieur le Ministre.'

Having kissed his son, Chevallier went upstairs with no word of kindness for his wife. He stripped to his trunks in the bedroom, and asked her to hand him clean linen. Yvonne demanded an explanation for his liaison with Jeanne. Chevallier replied with obscenities. He was going to marry Jeanne, he said, 'and you can remain in your own filth!' Amid the curses for his wife, he gloated over his appointment: 'I'm a minister!' he kept shouting.

Pierre remained unmoved when Yvonne fell sobbing to her knees and pleaded for a reconciliation. He called her worthless, he told her she stank, he piled insult upon insult. Finally, as she reached out pleading towards him, her hand brushed against his leg.

This was the catalyst. She had dared to *touch* the Under Secretary of State. Chevallier hurled a peculiarly foul-mouthed insult at his wife and made an especially obscene gesture.

Yvonne stiffened. She warned that if he went off with Jeanne she would kill herself. 'Go ahead,' he replied. 'It will be the first sensible thing you've done in your life.'

'I'm serious,' she cried, producing the automatic. 'I will kill myself.'

'Well, for God's sake kill yourself, but wait until I've gone.'

They were the last words Pierre Chevallier ever spoke. Yvonne came towards him firing as she walked: he was hit in leg, chin, chest and forehead. Having rushed downstairs to calm the crying Mathieu, she returned to the body in the bedroom. What happened next remains something of a mystery. By Yvonne's own account, she stooped over his body intending suicide. But thoughts of her children stayed her hand. As she rose from the corpse, the gun went off by accident and a fifth bullet lodged in his back.

France was outraged by the shooting. The war hero – the dynamic young mayor with his ministerial career just opening – had been cut down by what the

Pierre Chevallier

newspapers presented as a nagging wife. Feeling ran so high in Orléans itself that the trial was held in Rheims, far from the passions of the populace.

But when the case came to court, the mood changed. In part it was due to Yvonne and the tragic figure she made in the dock. Her face was a mask of suffering, the eyes dark and sunken from evident nights of anguish and remorse. Mechanically, she knotted and unknotted a handkerchief as the defence told of the humiliations she had endured. In contrast, the *soignée* elegance of Jeanne Perreau seemed almost an insult. Hissing was heard from the public benches as she gave evidence in the box. And Jeanne's husband, Léon Perreau, made a quite ridiculous impression as the *mari complaisant* in the case. It emerged that Jeanne had told him on the very first night that she had slept with Pierre. The affair had lasted 5 years, and throughout M. Perreau had been quite acquiescent. He had even been rather flattered to be cuckolded by the up-and-coming mayor. There were positive advantages too: Perreau's brother had been decorated with the Légion d'Honneur – on Chevallier's recommendation.

What a cosy arrangement for all concerned – except poor, suffering Yvonne. Public sympathy went out strongly to the deceived wife, and the prosecution sensed the climate of opinion. For example, the prisoner was not questioned about the mysterious fifth shot fired into the corpse. This could have been exploited at length as a possible act of malice and sacrilege. Nor did the prosecution make a ritual demand for the death penalty (as in the cases of Pauline Dubuisson and Léone Bouvier). It pressed instead for a short prison sentence, suggesting two years as an appropriate penalty.

The jury was out for less than an hour, one member asking for a point of clarification. The juror wanted to know precisely what was the obscene gesture that provoked Yvonne into reaching for the gun. The accused woman had broken into hysterical sobs when the question was asked during the trial; she had not been pressed at the time. Now, the authorities privately submitted an explicit description. It must have been thoroughly outrageous, for when the jury returned it acquitted Yvonne Chevallier of every charge against her. She left the court a free woman, cheered by a large crowd outside.

Although fully exonerated for her tragic action, Yvonne Chevallier selected a punishment for herself. A few months after the trial, she took herself and her two sons off to the benighted settlement at St Laurent du Maroni. This had been the site of one of France's notorious penal colonies in the mosquito swamps of French Guiana. The prison was closed, but a ramshackle community of natives and French settlers still lived there.

Banishing herself to that tropical hell, Yvonne Chevallier took up the post of a sister in charge of the maternity wing of the hospital. She was trained for the job. Yvonne had been a midwife before meeting Pierre and participating in his brilliant career.

Tess and the Wessex Hanging

She is the most moving of all Thomas Hardy's doomed heroines. Bright-eyed, peony-mouthed Tess of the d'Urbervilles is an innocent dairy maid seduced by a young man of means. Later, caught in a love triangle from which she sees no issue, Tess murders her seducer to liberate herself. Tried and condemned to death without reprieve she dies on the scaffold, a tragic sport of the gods.

Hardy drew on the country girls of his native Wessex when he painted her portrait; there was no one model for Tess. But a macabre event from his childhood provided the emotional inspiration for the novel, perhaps darkening the whole of his work. On 9 August 1856, young Thomas Hardy saw a woman hanged. Her name was Martha Brown and, like Tess, she was a victim of the eternal triangle.

Hardy was only 16 at the time. But the impression was to stay with him for the rest of his life. In 1925, when in his eighties, the novelist was to write of the execution: 'I remember what a fine figure she showed against the sky as she hung in the misty rain, and how the tight black silk gown set off her shape as she wheeled half-round and back.'

There is more than a trace of morbid sensuality in the passage; we can only guess what effect the experience may have had on the adolescent's awakening sexual impulses. The condemned woman's face had been hooded but the material, wet with rain, permitted her face to be seen quite clearly. This evidently haunted the novelist. He wrote: 'I saw – they had put a cloth over her face – how, as the cloth got wet, her features came through it. That was *extraordinary*.'

Tess, of course, has been made the subject of films, plays – and even an Italian opera by d'Erlanger. Martha Brown's story is not so well known. And yet it caused quite a sensation in its day.

Elizabeth Martha Brown was a handsome woman who lived at Birdsmoorgate, near Beaminster in Dorset. She was some 20 years older than her husband John Brown, a carrier by trade. He, it was whispered, had only married her for her money and he certainly had a roving eye. For one day in 1856, Martha caught him making love to another woman. Late that night the couple had a furious row at their home. John Brown struck his wife with his carrier's whip, and she responded by seizing an axe. The blow proved fatal.

HELL HATH NO FURY

In France, Martha Brown might have gone to trial confident of securing an acquittal. It was a classic domestic *crime passionnel*, in which sympathy for the outraged wife would surely have won leniency. But a sterner morality prevailed in Victorian Dorset. And the accused woman made matters very much worse by trying to conceal the crime. She claimed that her husband had been killed by a kick from his horse – a falsehood in which she persisted throughout her trial. It was only at the end that she confessed to having wielded the axe herself.

By then it was too late. She was condemned to death and despite immense public interest, the Home Secretary refused to grant a reprieve.

Thomas Hardy

THE WORLD'S GREATEST CRIMES OF PASSION

A crowd of some three or four thousand gathered at Dorchester Gaol to attend the hanging. Rain was falling, and a certain nervousness seems to have afflicted the officials. No woman had been hung there for some time, and the prison chaplain was too overcome with emotion to accompany Martha to the scaffold. A young clergyman was brought in to deputize (his name was Henry Moule and he was, as it happened, a friend of the Hardy family).

The public executioner, a man named Calcraft, was supposed to tie the condemned woman's dress around her so that it did not ride up to expose her as she dropped. Being out of practice, he forgot this item of procedure. Having made his way down to operate the trap, he had to climb the scaffold again.

Through all the grim preparations, Martha Brown remained calm and dignified. She had shaken hands firmly with the prison authorities before being led up the steps. And she waited in silence for the ordeal.

Young Thomas Hardy saw it all. He was apprenticed, at the time, to a Dorchester architect, and obtained a very close view of the gallows by climbing a tree close to the gaol's entrance. His second wife was to suggest that the episode tinged his life's work with bitterness and gloom. But Hardy's own references to it betray a ghoulish relish rather than melancholy. It was, no doubt, the same relish that had drawn the other thousands to the scene. In old age he professed to being ashamed of attending the hanging, 'my only excuse being that I was but a youth.'

Certainly the case fascinated him, and there is no question that the image of the condemned woman was with him as he planned his Tess. For in his personal scrapbook he kept a newspaper cutting in which a friend discussed the influence of the event on his most famous novel. Hardy pencilled in some corrections to minor points of detail (the text said that Martha had used a knife, for example). But he let the claims regarding Tess stand. And he also left the following:

> He never forgot the rustle of the thin black gown the woman was wearing as she was led forth by the warders. A penetrating rain was falling; the white cap was no sooner over the woman's head than it clung to her features, and the noose was put round the neck of what looked like a marble statue. Hardy looked at the scene with the strange illusion of its being unreal, and was brought to his complete senses when the drop fell with a thud and his companion on a lower branch of the tree fell fainting to the ground.

Hardy's boyhood companion was not alone in feeling the horror of the event. The execution provoked a leading article in the *Dorset County Chronicle*, which called for an end to the death penalty. And though it was over a hundred years before capital punishment was finally abolished in Britain, local sensitivities had clearly been aroused. For after the hanging of Martha Brown, there were no more public executions in Dorchester.

Delayed Action

Postwar France had no sympathy for collaborators. Most of the population had submitted to the German invaders, and resistance – at least until the last months of the war – was much more limited than is often supposed. Nevertheless, people who had actively assisted the Germans learned to tremble after the D-Day landings. They lived in terror of the midnight knock, of strangers at their door – of the fatal shots.

For girls who had gone out with German soldiers, a ritual humiliation was reserved. They had their heads shaved and were paraded through the streets to face the kicks, spittle and jeers of the populace. Pauline Dubuisson knew the ordeal; her head too had been shaved.

Her father was a successful engineer who lived in Dunkirk, scene of the famous beach evacuation. An admirer of Nietzsche's philosophy and of the authoritarian Nazi regime, he willingly undertook building contracts for the Germans. He brought Pauline up in a hard school. She was taught to think much and to feel little.

Pauline was only 13 when France fell, but soon she was flirting with enemy soldiers. At 17 she was mistress to a 55-year-old German colonel, and was listed by the Resistance as a collaborator. The price was paid after the Allied landings. Pauline was dragged into the main square and forced onto a stool while the men sheered off her long black hair.

Still, she had her whole life ahead of her. In 1946, the year after all hostilities ended, Pauline enrolled as a medical student at the University of Lille. Her first year report described her as intelligent, even brilliant at times, 'but she is not a steady worker. She is well balanced but haughty, provoking and a flirt. Her conduct is mediocre.'

It was at Lille that Pauline first met a handsome and athletic young student named Félix Bailly, who came from St Omer. They had a tempestuous three-year affair in which Pauline repeatedly cuckolded her lover, sleeping with other students and members of the faculty. Félix offered to marry her; it was Pauline who refused. She continued to behave promiscuously, even keeping a notebook in which she recorded details of her different lovers' performances. In the end, Félix decided to break with her. He left Lille and went to Paris to continue his medical course there.

What happened – or rather, what didn't happen – next, played a key part in the coming controversy. For some 18 months the couple saw nothing of each other. Félix settled down to his work as a diligent, well-liked student. And he also

23

became engaged to a beautiful fair-haired young woman named Monique Lombard. Back in Lille, meanwhile, Pauline was as promiscuous as ever. She even arranged a summer holiday in Germany where she resumed her friendship with the former German colonel. She made no attempt to contact Félix. Not until 1951.

Early in March of that year, a mutual friend who had been to Paris learned of Félix's marriage plans. Back in Lille Pauline heard all about the beautiful blonde and the happy future which beckoned Félix. She immediately went to Paris to meet her former lover, and try to rekindle his affections, but it didn't work. Something must have snapped then. On 10 March Pauline went back to Dunkirk to celebrate her birthday. Her father gave her 5,000 francs and with it, having acquired a fire-arms licence, she went out and bought a little .25 calibre automatic.

Pauline did not head straight for Paris. She first returned to Lille where she penned a note declaring her intention of killing both Félix and herself. The landlady had noticed the gun in her handbag, and after Pauline took the Paris train, she also discovered the threatening note. Realising the terrible danger Félix was in, the landlady telephoned Félix's father and sent a warning telegram to Félix himself.

It was less than a fortnight before his wedding was due. Félix recognised the peril, and on the night of 15 March he stayed away from his small apartment on the Left Bank, preferring to stop over at the flat of a friend, Georges Gaudel. The next night he did return to his apartment, but with Gaudel with him to act as a guardian. They were having breakfast together there on the morning of 17 March when a knock was heard at the door. It was Pauline.

She said that she wanted to see Félix alone; impossible, he replied, he had a friend with him. She persisted: 'I want to be alone with you, just for a moment . . .'

'Why alone?'

'Because I'm afraid of crying.'

Félix refused to admit her. But he did cautiously agree to a meeting in a public place, as long as Gaudel was present. They chose the Place Cambronne as a suitable site and arranged to meet there in three-quarters of an hour. Pauline left, and so in due course did Félix with Gaudel at his side.

However anguished Pauline may have been – with jealousy, despair or pure malice – there is no question that her brain now calculated with the utmost coolness and clarity. She never went to the Place Cambronne at all. Instead, she found a vantage point in a café opposite Félix's flat. There she sat and she waited, watching as the two men left, with a drink before her on the table.

Félix and Gaudel spent a nervous hour at the Place Cambronne, expecting Pauline at any moment. Eventually, though, Félix considered the danger over and decided to return to his flat. Gaudel, he said, could make his own arrangements for the day. But the companion was not so reassured. He insisted they phone another friend Bernard Mougeot to take over the role of guardian.

The call was made and Mougeot agreed to go to Félix's flat immediately. It seemed that they had covered every possible peril and Félix returned to the flat.

He was expecting Mougeot to be there already. But fate had determined otherwise. There was a transport strike in Paris that day, and the hurrying friend's taxi got stuck in a traffic jam. Pauline watched as her ex-lover returned alone to the apartment block. She paid for her coffee and followed him to the seventh floor where his flat was situated.

It is not certain how she gained admittance; probably, Félix heard a knock and assumed that Mougeot had arrived. What is beyond doubt is that Pauline shot her ex-lover three times. Any of the wounds could have killed him. The third bullet was apparently a cool *coup de grâce* delivered behind the right ear.

Pauline then tried to shoot herself too, but the gun jammed on the fourth bullet. Instead, she disconnected the pipe in the kitchen which led to the gas stove. Placing the free end in her mouth, she lay down and prepared for death.

It was some time before Bernard Mougeot arrived. He could smell the gas in the corridor and hurried in to find his friend weltering in blood on the living-room floor. Pauline, in the kitchen, was unconscious. Mougeot pulled the pipe from her mouth and summoned the fire brigade. They arrived quickly and managed to revive her with oxygen cylinders.

Pauline recovered in hospital. But the case was to claim another victim before it came to court. In Dunkirk, Pauline's father discovered what had happened. While the family discussed which lawyer to hire, he came to a decision of his own. Declaring the shame to be unendurable, he wrote a letter expressing grief and commiseration to Félix's parents. Then, having taken a dose of poison for good measure, he gassed himself in the kitchen. M. Dubuisson's will triumphed where Pauline's had failed. He was dead when they found him there.

It was many months before Pauline's trial came up in Paris. The date was set for 28 October 1952, but on that morning she was discovered unconscious in her cell, bleeding from her wrist. She had managed to open a vein with a needle and a splinter of glass. A suicide note, apparently written in the dark after her wrist was cut, expressed both regret for the crime and disdain for the coming trial: 'I think my family is accursed and myself also. I only hurt those whom I love most in the world. I have already lost over a litre of blood but I am still all right . . .'

Again revived, she was brought to trial a month later amid intense public interest. The *crime passionnel* is, of course, something of a French speciality. But the case of Pauline Dubuisson did not fit the classic pattern. The problem for the jurors and the fascinated public alike revolved around the timespan involved. Could jealous love really be quickened 18 months after the liaison was over? Or

25

had Pauline acted purely out of malice: indifferent to Félix while she possessed him, wrathful when he sought happiness elsewhere?

The stigma of her wartime past inevitably weighed against her. She could scarcely be represented as an injured lover. If there was a woman in court to be pitied it was surely the beautiful Monique Lombard, bereaved fiancée of the murder victim. She appeared pitifully in the witness box, and the prosecutor at one point compared her innocent love with the malevolence of (pointing dramatically at Pauline) 'this bitch!'

The prosecution called for the death penalty, and pursued its case savagely. Even Pauline's suicide attempts were scorned. How convenient, it was insinuated, that the gun jammed before Pauline could shoot herself. Had she really tried to gas herself? Or did she turn the tap only when she heard the sound of someone arriving at the door? Remarkable, was it not, that she should have failed yet again when she cut her wrist. 'You are more efficient when it comes to murder', taunted the prosecutor.

The thrusts were vicious – and surely unfair. The murder weapon was found jammed on the fourth shot. Firemen testified that Pauline had second-degree asphyxiation when they arrived: she was foaming at the lips. And she had lost over a litre of blood when discovered in her cell.

But Pauline's character was such that things looked very black for her. Extracts from the notebook in which she described her lovers' performances were read out in court. The passages concerning Félix and her other lovers too were cold and acid in tone. In the dock she remained largely unmoved by others' grief – everyone noted the 'mask of pride' that she wore. To win an acquittal, the defence had to prove the case to be a *crime passionnel*. What did Pauline Dubuisson know of love?

Might she even go to the guillotine? No woman had been executed in France during peacetime since 1887. On that occasion, a writhing female victim had to be dragged under the blade by her hair. The episode was so sickening that the public executioner threatened to resign if any more women were brought before him. A convention had since developed, whereby even if a woman was sentenced to death, she would always be granted a reprieve.

If Pauline were found guilty of murder, would the convention hold? Perhaps there was a trace of doubt in the jury's mind, for they brought in a verdict of murder – but without premeditation. She was sentenced to penal servitude for life.

A curious verdict. Her behaviour for days before the shooting suggested that she had murder very much in mind. A curious sentence, too. For a more orthodox *crime passionnel* she might have expected much more lenient treatment.

Clearly this was a killing with an extenuating circumstance. It is hard to know how to define it, – unless you called it delayed-action love.

A Tale of Two Sisters

Chronic alcoholism is a deep-rooted problem in the French countryside. Wine is cheap and the hard routines of farming life can be monotonous. To escape them, many a working man daily stupefies his senses with the bottle. M. Bouvier of Saint-Macaire came from a long line of hereditary alcoholics. His special drink was not wine, as it happens, but a crude cider alcohol distilled in the region of western France where he lived. Bouvier used to get violently drunk and regularly threatened to murder his wife and two daughters. From an early age, the girls learned to help their mother with the almost nightly ordeal of strapping him down to the bed. Someone would then run for the doctor. The doctor would give him the injections that brought a fragile calm to the household.

This is the story of those two sisters. Georgette, the older one, plays only a peripheral role in the drama. Yet it was to be intensely significant in the life of Léone, the younger girl.

The village of Saint-Macaire lies near the town of Cholet in the Maine-et-Loire department. And at the local school, Georgette showed considerable intelligence. At the age of 18 she managed to escape the household by entering a convent at Angers. Forsaking the hell of her family life, she submitted to the pious disciplines of a nun's existence. And there, for a while, we must leave her.

Léone Bouvier, two years younger, cried for a week when her sister abandoned the household. She was alone now with the wreck of her father and a mother who had also taken to drinking. Léone was not bright; in fact, her school years had left her practically illiterate. The meagre salary she earned at a local shoe factory was absorbed by the family's needs. But her mother showed no gratitude. She mocked Léone for being worthless and dull-witted. And, rejected by all those closest to her, Léone looked for love elsewhere. She turned, in particular, to men.

She was not a pretty girl. Her eyes were wide-set, her nose was large and a ragged shank of dark hair fell across her low brow. A generous heart only made her an easier prey for the local lads.

Léone lost her virginity to a fellow factory worker at a hurried coupling in the corner of a field. She saw him the next day, laughing about the episode with his mates in the factory yard. Other sad encounters were to follow until she struck up with a decent-hearted young man in the Air Force. Fate never gave Léone a break, though; not long after they arranged to be married, the youth was killed in an accident.

27

THE WORLD'S GREATEST CRIMES OF PASSION

It was in the bleak period following the incident that Léone met Emile Clenet, a 22-year-old garage mechanic from Nantes. Their first brief encounter was at a dance in Cholet, and they made a rendezvous for the following afternoon. Misfortune was Léone's constant companion, and while cycling to the meeting she had to stop to fix a puncture. By the time she arrived, he was gone.

Six months later, however, they met again at the Lent carnival in Cholet. 'You're six months late,' joked Emile. 'But never mind, we've found each other again.' They enjoyed all the fun of the fair together and afterwards, Emile took her to a hotel room. She had never been treated to clean sheets before. She learned to love him then.

The couple fell into a set pattern of meetings. To reverse the lyrics of the popular song, it was 'Only on a Sunday' for Emile and Léone. He was a hard worker and reserved only the seventh day for his pleasures. Every Sunday, Léone would cycle to a particular spot near Cholet, and Emile would pick her up on his motorbike. After picnicing and perhaps some evening dancing, they would retire to a cheap hotel.

There was talk of marriage, and Emile took her home to meet his parents, who rather liked their son's strange little girlfriend. It is hard to determine exactly what went wrong. Perhaps Emile never seriously intended marriage. Once, there was an accident with his motorbike and Léone took a knock on the head. She suffered headaches and bouts of depression after that.

Emile could be cruel, too. Once, snapped by a street photographer, the couple went to pick up the picture. Emile took one look and said he didn't want it. When Léone asked why, he said: 'Just look at that face and you'll understand.' She hurried off to cry alone. Since meeting Emile, Léone had been taking care of her appearance, indulging in all the feminine vanities. Words like those must have wounded deeply.

The real blow came when she found she was pregnant and Emile told her to get rid of the unborn child. She did so – but the headaches and depressions grew worse after that. Then, in January 1952, she lost her job. There was a furious row in her home that night: her mother raged at her and her drunken father tried to give her a thrashing. Léone fled the household. It took her all night to cycle the 30-odd miles to Nantes where Emile worked. But when she got there in the morning, Emile was annoyed. Their arrangement was only for Sundays, he said. It was a weekday. She must leave.

Utterly abandoned, Léone spent two weeks as an outcast in Nantes, wandering the cold, winter streets. A second attempt to see Emile resulted in another rebuff. He said he was too busy to see her for the next couple of Sundays. Her money ran out. She had nowhere to sleep. And though she was never very clear about what happened during that blank fortnight, it seems she slipped into prostitution.

During the days, Léone took to standing outside gun-shop windows, gazing dazedly in at the gleaming butts and barrels. Later, she was to say that she did not quite know why she did so; perhaps suicide had been in her mind. But she remembered one incident very clearly. As she stood there, shivering in the rain, a strange young man had appeared at her side. 'Don't', said the figure, 'He is too young. He has the right to live.' Then he disappeared.

Hallucination? Léone had been a victim all her life, and perhaps her conscious mind was moving towards thoughts of self-destruction. But perhaps, too, some last instinct to survive and strike outward was prompting from within. The impulse was to murder her lover. And to redress the balance, her conscience invented the phantasmagoric young man who seemed to know her thoughts.

Whatever the truth, that voice seems to have earned Emile a reprieve. For she did not yet buy a gun. Instead, physically and emotionally exhausted, she returned to her village. Nothing had changed there. On arrival, her father was in one of his frenzies. Mechanically, she helped her mother strap him to the bed.

She had come back from one hell to another, and only thoughts of Emile sustained her. 15 February 1952 was Léone's 23rd birthday. Would her lover remember? Last year he had bought her a bicycle lamp – the only present of her adult life. She summoned up her courage, took the last of her savings, and boarded the coach back to Nantes. Humbly and apologetically she approached him at the garage and asked if they could meet on Sunday at the usual place. He showed no sign of remembering her birthday. But – to her intense joy – he agreed to meet at the rendezvous.

When he came, he brought no birthday present. Emile made love brusquely that Sunday and he did not stay the night as usual. It was on the following day that Léone went into Nantes and sought out one of the gunshops. There she bought a .22 automatic. The pistol had recently been declared a 'sporting weapon'. Léone, who could barely sign her name, did not need a license.

She lived now only for their Sundays. Léone hung around in Nantes waiting for the next meeting, living from day to day in the dockside area by taking men into hotel bedrooms. When the grey haze of waiting hours was over she hastened

---

To Have And To Hold
On 27 August 1984, Mrs Jose Kubiczek returned to her home at Saint-Amand-les-Eaux. It was to be a final visit; she came only to take custody of her son. But it seems her husband could not face the future without her. The French police reported he had strangled his wife, then dressed her in a wedding gown. He was found lying beside her corpse on the conjugal bed.

to their rendezvous at Cholet. Emile was not there. She scoured the town and eventually found his motorbike parked outside a cinema. When the film was over she ran to meet him, but he brushed her off. He had flu, he said. He was going straight home. She must wait for the coming Lent carnival.

Fate, which had dogged Léone all her life, had reserved its completing irony for this meeting. It was at Cholet's Lent carnival that the couple had enjoyed their first night together two years earlier. It was at the Lent carnival too, with its hurdy-gurdy gaiety, that Léone Bouvier was to kill her lover.

Yet it started so well. Emile roared up on his motorbike at their rendezvous and she mounted pillion on the back just as in the old days. She kissed him as they rode into the town centre to mingle with the carnival crowds. They moved gaily among the stalls, the streamers and the balloons. Emile stopped by a shooting range to demonstrate his prowess. The weapon (fate again) was a .22 automatic. And above the staccato crackle of gunshot he told her he was leaving to work in North Africa. He was going, he said, for good.

'But what about me? We were going to get married . . .'

'So what?'

'You don't want to marry me any more, then?'

'C'est la vie.' Emile shrugged and mumbled platitudes, telling her she would find someone better than him. Léone was incredulous. She asked again. Again he said no, he would never marry her.

Emile drove her back to her bicycle, locked up at their rendezvous. There she implored him, 'Emile, you aren't going off and leaving me like this?'

Emile said nothing, but returned to his motorcycle and climbed on, preparing to leave. Léone took the gun from her handbag and slipped it under her coat. She came up behind him. 'Emile,' she whispered, 'kiss me for the last time . . .'

He did not respond. She put her left arm around his neck and pulled him tenderly towards her. Gently, she kissed his cheek. And as she did so she withdrew the pistol and placed the barrel-end against his neck. Then she pulled the trigger.

There was only one shot.

Afterwards she mounted her bicycle and fled, pedalling blindly to the only place she knew that offered sanctuary. It was to Angers that she cycled, to her sister's convent. She arrived there in distress, without explaining what had happened. Georgette gave her coffee and put her to bed – the poor, ruined child come like a ghost from her past.

The police came the following afternoon. Léone was arrested in the convent, but such are the procedures of French law that it was not until December 1953 that she was brought before the Assizes of Maine-et-Loire. French courts are traditionally flexible in the handling of a *crime passionnel*. Léone's misfortune was to face an unusually aggressive prosecutor and a hostile judge.

Judges play a more active role in the French courts than their English equivalents do. They may examine and cross-question a defendant at some length. And at Léone's trial in Angers, the judge showed himself entirely lacking in the subtlety associated with the French legal mind. What he had in abundance was the stubborn hypocrisy of the French provincial bourgeois.

He simply could not see that Léone's blighted childhood or her lover's callous rebuffs made one jot of difference to the case. Why did she not stay at her parents' hearth instead of wandering the dockside at Nantes? The answer should have been evident when Léone's father was brought to the witness box, sweating and shaking under the ordeal of a morning without a drink. The experts declared him an hereditary alcoholic. The mother, too, frankly admitted that they had all lived in mortal fear of his violence. But she explained that she'd done the best she could, adding the fateful reflection that her other daughter was a nun.

The judge pounced.

'You see!' he called, rounding on Léone, 'There was no need for you to go wrong. Why did you go wrong?' It is hard to exaggerate the part played by this circumstance. It seemed to nullify every mitigating factor of Léone's background. The writer Derrick Goodman has made the point eloquently: they did not come down hard on Léone because she had murdered her lover. It was because her sister was a nun.

The judge continued with his tirade, dwelling on the fact that Léone had killed Emile as she kissed him. This was a detail that seemed to him an incomprehensible outrage: '*atroce!*' he fumed, '*atroce!*'

Léone stood quietly in the dock, her head bowed low.

'Why did you kill him?' demanded the judge.

Tears were streaming down her cheeks as Léone raised her head.

'I loved him', she said simply.

The prosecution had called for the death penalty on the charge of premeditated murder. For reasons stated in the case of Pauline Dubuisson, there was no likelihood of Léone being executed. In fact, the defence had every right to expect a very lenient judgement. What was Léone's crime if not a *crime passionnel*? Middle-class ladies had walked scot-free in cases of this nature.

The jury was out for only a quarter of an hour. And it would seem that they arrived at the same formula as in the case of Pauline Dubuisson. They avoided the charge of premeditated murder, for that carried an automatic death penalty, and found her guilty of murder – but without premeditation.

The foreman complacently suggested that the prisoner be given the maximum penalty of penal servitude for life – a minimum of 20 years. The judge readily agreed. And so, with the afflictions of a simple mind and a warm heart, a horrific childhood and a succession of rejections, Léone Bouvier fell victim to the full weight of French law.

The Real Mrs Mainwaring

The town of Colditz in Upper Saxony is remembered today for its castle, built high above the River Mulde, which housed some of the most determined escapers of World War Two. But long before its masonry knew the silent excavations of the Allied POWs, that brooding silhouette had looked down on a drama of a very different kind.

It was to Colditz that, in the summer of 1871, there came an English gentleman named Mainwaring with a beautiful companion that everyone took to be his young wife. Mainwaring booked in at a well known hotel, and engaged a suite of apartments for his honeymoon. He even received letters there, postmarked from Ferrybridge in Yorkshire. All, it appears, went on as merry as a marriage bell until one day an Englishwoman, travelling incognito, arrived at the hotel, taking two rooms on the same floor as the loving couple.

Her name was Mrs Mainwaring.

For a day or two, the real Mrs Mainwaring bided her time, apparently maturing her plan for revenge. Then, one night, she crept stealthily along the passage leading to her husband's bedchamber. Entering, pistol in hand, she saw her husband and his partner together among the sheets. Without a second thought she levelled the gun and fired. The ball passed through Mr Mainwaring's head – he died almost instantly.

This classic Victorian drama of love and vengeance had a fittingly tragic outcome. The real Mrs Mainwaring, her 'fell purpose' accomplished, was duly arrested and taken to prison. However, she was found dead in her cell the next morning. According to *The Illustrated Police News* which reported the story, she had managed to conceal poison about her person and must have swallowed it soon after her incarceration. The doctors were unanimous in their opinion that she had been dead for several hours.

The Bigamists
Bigamy provides one way out of a love triangle. In one scandalous Victorian case, the Earl of Euston sought divorce from the Countess of Euston on the grounds that she had a husband living when she married. But it emerged at the trial that the husband in question had a wife living when he married her. The Earl was refused his divorce on the grounds that the Countess was free.

A Life for a Life

Early in July 1955, north country publican Albert Pierrepoint received official notice that he would be needed in London on the 13th. A small, tidy man, Pierrepoint made the appropriate arrangements for a journey he had made many times before. On the afternoon of 12 July he arrived at the gates of Holloway Prison in North London. Admitted by the authorities, he was given a cup of tea and then taken to the door of a cell where, through the peep-hole, he could see a pale young woman reading a Bible.

The officials supplied the statistics he needed to know: Height – 5 ft 2 inches; Weight – 103 lbs. Albert Pierrepoint, official hangman, studied her file and proceeded to the execution chamber where, using a sandbag for dummy, he tested the spring-loaded mechanism of the trap.

At 09.00 the following morning, 28-year-old Ruth Ellis entered the chamber to become the last woman hanged in Britain. She faced the noose with the same extraordinary calm as she had exhibited throughout her trial and her ordeal of waiting. Ruth Ellis asked neither for sympathy nor for mercy. From the condemned cell she had written, 'I say a life for a life.'

The hanging was efficiently accomplished. The post mortem noted the fractures to spine, thyroid and cartilage, but reported the air passages clear. She had not been strangled like so many before her: 'No engorgement . . . No asphyxial changes . . . Cause of Death: Injuries to the central nervous system consequent upon judicial hanging.'

Yet neither the prisoner's calm, Pierrepoint's expertise, nor any amount of paperwork could mask the essential horror of what had transpired. 1955 was the year when Rock'n'Roll hit Britain; the first year of commercial television. Yet at Holloway Prison, an Old Testament form of tribal retribution had been enacted upon Ruth Ellis. For days beforehand, friends, relatives, lawyers and MPs had been pressing desperately for a reprieve. On the eve of the execution, the crowds had already started to assemble outside the prison gates, equipped with Thermos flasks and sleeping bags, so as to be near as the macabre drama was played out. Among them was a vociferous minority chanting for the abolition of a penalty which seemed more barbarous than murder itself. The hanging of Ruth Ellis did not only shock because the condemned woman was young and blonde and attractive. It exposed an iron inflexibility in the British legal system. Even in 1955, there was hardly another country in the civilised world where a crime of passion was punishable on the scaffold.

Born Ruth Hornby at Rhyl in 1926, the condemned woman had led a chequered life. At 15 she had escaped from a difficult home background to start work as a waitress. In due course she found employment at a munitions factory and was already dyeing her hair with the peroxide that was to distinguish her in all the press photographs. Ruth was no shy maiden. With a slender, somewhat predatory sensuality she found it easy to acquire dancing partners among servicemen at the wartime clubs she began to frequent in London. In 1944 she had a child by a Canadian soldier, and no sooner had her figure returned than she took up a job as nude model in a Camera Club. In the years of postwar austerity, West End vice lords were already spinning their webs of sleazy excitement. Ruth became a club hostess and call girl. In 1950 she married George Ellis, an alcoholic dentist who frequented her low-life locales. The couple had a daughter but separated soon afterwards, and Ruth returned to the circuit. It was while working as manageress at the Little Club, a seedy upstairs drinking room in Knightsbridge, that she met David Blakely, the man she was to murder.

Blakely came from a very different background. Born in 1929, the son of a well-to-do Sheffield doctor, he was given a public school education at Shrewsbury, and throughout his brief life he retained his boyish good looks. Blakely remained immature in temperament too. For all his suave charm and his well-bred accent, he never held down a steady job. Feckless, emotionally vulnerable and prone to sulks, Blakely maintained abiding enthusiasms only for alcohol, for women and – above all – for racing cars. When he drank he became obstreperous, provoking fights he was too cowardly to see through. With his women he was a braggart and a largely unsuccessful lover. And his experiences on the motor circuits were hardly any happier.

Blakely raced at Silverstone and other well-known tracks, including Le Mans in France. But though he consorted at clubs and meetings with stars like Mike Hawthorne and Stirling Moss, victory almost always eluded him. Nor did racing offer him a career. His obsession for cars, as for drink and women, was financed chiefly by private money, including a £7,000 legacy from his father.

Blakely first met Ruth Ellis in 1953. The young racing driver was drunk and insulting on that occasion, and Ruth referred to him afterwards as a 'pompous ass', telling a friend, 'I hope never to see that little shit again.' But she did – with consequences disastrous to both.

Blakely took to frequenting the Little Club, where Ruth succumbed to his charm and expensive manners. David was 'class', and before long they were sleeping together at her flat above the premises. Ruth, at the outset, was clearly the dominant partner, confident and self-possessed while he was weak and ineffectual. Moreover, as Blakely frittered away more and more of his resources, he came to depend on her to subsidise his drinking.

After having a child of Blakely's aborted in December 1953, Ruth tried to cool

Ruth Ellis

the relationship by cultivating a more dependable lover, company director Desmond Cussen. At about the same time she lost her job at the Little Club, partly because of the time and money she had expended on David.

Ruth first moved into Cussen's apartment, and later to a flat at Egerton Gardens. Cussen loaned her the rent and was a frequent visitor there. But Ruth could not entirely break with her younger lover. She continued to sleep with Blakely, who eventually moved in with her at Egerton Gardens. It was a period of savage quarrels and recriminations between Ruth and David. He was intensely jealous, drank heavily, and sometimes beat Ruth so badly that she had to use make-up to camouflage the livid bruises on her limbs. She had a second abortion by him, and under the strain of the tempestuous relationship consulted a doctor who prescribed tranquillisers for her depression. Blakely, meanwhile, had invested what little capital he possessed in building a racing car. Predictably, the vehicle broke down in practice before its racing debut.

What bonded Ruth to her young lover? Love? Social ambition, or his periodic promises of marriage? Blakely had become a liability to Ruth, yet during this period of frenzied passion, the see-saw of emotional need began to tilt. Blakely had not lost his middle-class expectations, and to friends of his, a married couple called the Findlaters, he confided his despair and his own need to make a break with Ruth Ellis. Ruth had long suspected that David was having an affair with Mrs Findlater, and the more time he spent in the company of the married couple, the more her own jealousy quickened. Ruth could dish out violence as well as take it; once, it seems, she slashed Blakely in the back with a knife.

Things came to a head at Easter, 1955. On Good Friday, 8 April, Blakely confessed to the Findlaters that he was getting frightened of Ruth. They suggested he spend the weekend with them at their apartment in Tanza Road, Hampstead. Though he was due to meet Ruth at 19.30 that night, Blakely gratefully accepted.

For two hours, Ruth waited at Egerton Gardens for her lover to turn up. At 21.30 she phoned the Findlaters to find out if David was there. The au pair took the call and told her that neither Blakely nor the Findlaters were in the flat. An hour later, Ruth phoned again, and this time Anthony Findlater answered. Though he claimed to know nothing of her lover's whereabouts, Ruth did not believe him. Again and again that night she rang Tanza Road, and in the end Findlater simply hung up the receiver whenever her voice came on the line. At the trial it was learned that Blakely was indeed at Tanza Road – shaking with fear on the couch.

Frenzied with suspicion, Ruth had Desmond Cussen drive her round to Tanza Road. When she saw Blakely's green Vanguard parked outside the flat, she ran in fury to the front door and repeatedly rang the bell. No-one replied. Eventually, she vented her spleen on the Vanguard, thumping in its side

The Hangman's Verdict
For hanging Ruth Ellis, Albert Pierrepoint collected a fee of fifteen guineas (plus travelling expenses). He left Holloway practically besieged by a storming mob and needed police protection to get through. Pierrepoint returned to his pub, the Rose and Crown at Hoole, near Preston, and the wife who had never asked questions. And there he came to a decision: he would give up his macabre profession.

His had been an hereditary vocation, his father and uncle both having been listed as qualified executioners on the Home Office files. When the press learned of his resignation, it was rumoured that something exceptionally grim must have transpired in the death chamber. It had not – Ruth Ellis was 'the bravest woman I ever hanged' and there was 'nothing untoward'. Pierrepoint resigned because the furore caused him to examine his own conscience. Did hanging really deter murder? He concluded that it did not: 'Capital punishment, in my view, achieved nothing except revenge.'

windows which were held in place only by rubber strips. The glass did not break, but the noise brought Anthony Findlater to the door in his pajamas.

There was a furious scene in the street where Ruth kept demanding that Blakely come down, and Findlater denied that he was there. Already, the married couple had prudently phoned for the police. An inspector turned up and tried to calm the situation; after warning Ruth against breaching the peace he drove away.

Findlater slammed the door, leaving Ruth still fulminating in the street. Nor did she leave at once, but kept prowling around the Vanguard until a second police visit forced her from the scene. The long-suffering Desmond Cussen, who had waited and watched throughout the whole performance, drove her back to Egerton Gardens.

His role in the affair deserves a word of explanation. Cussen was infatuated with Ruth but, lacking David's youth and glamour, knew he must wait until the flame of her earlier love was extinguished. For that reason, it appears, he was prepared to acquiesce with Ruth in what became an ever more obsessive quest.

Ruth did not sleep that night. Early the next morning she took a taxi to Tanza Road and kept watch on the Findlaters' from a darkened doorway. At about 10.00 Findlater emerged, and beckoned Blakely out into the street. Having

David Blakely

examined the damaged car, the two men got in and drove off down the road.

Ruth's suspicions were confirmed – the Findlaters *were* shielding David from her. Armed with this certainty, she spent the next hours in attempts to track down her lover's movements. After lunch, she and Cussen took her ten-year-old son to the London Zoo, leaving him there with enough money for the afternoon. Then, with Cussen as chauffeur, she continued the hunt for her quarry.

Cussen drove her back to Hampstead where they located the now-repaired Vanguard outside the Magdala public house. After considerably more furtive reconnoitring, they returned to Ruth's flat, gave her son his supper and put him to bed. That night, Cussen again drove her to Tanza Road where the Findlaters were holding a small party. Listening from the street, Ruth could hear David's voice – and a woman giggling at his remarks. A new suspicion took root in Ruth's fevered mind. David was not pursuing an affair with Mrs Findlater – but with the couple's au pair! A trivial occurrence seemed to confirm this idea: at a certain point, the blinds went down in what Ruth took to be the girl's bedroom; and at the same time, she ceased to hear David's voice. The Findlaters, Ruth convinced herself, were using the au pair to prise her young lover away from her.

Cussen drove Ruth home at about 21.00, and she spent a second sleepless night, chain-smoking and nursing her mute fury. By the following evening, on Easter Sunday, she must have been practically unhinged. 'I was very upset', she acknowledged at her trial. 'I had a peculiar feeling I wanted to kill him.'

By her own account, Ruth Ellis made her way by taxi to Hampstead that evening. In her handbag she carried a heavy .38 Smith and Wesson revolver. Arriving at Tanza Road she saw no sign of the Vanguard, so she made her way on foot to the Magdala pub where she sighted David's car by the kerb. Peering through the windows of the hostelry, she could see David and a friend, Mayfair car salesman Clive Gunnell, drinking at the bar. In fact, the two men had only come to replenish stocks for an evening at Tanza Road. Having downed their drinks, they came out into the street carrying cigarettes and three quarts of light ale.

Neither noticed Ruth at first. With a quart of beer under his arm, David approached the Vanguard, fumbling in his pocket for the keys.

'David!' she called, but he did not seem to hear. Ruth approached, taking the revolver from her bag. 'David!' she called again, and this time he turned to see the blonde with the Smith and Wesson.

Immediately, he ran towards the back of the van. Two shots echoed in quick succession. Blakely was slammed against the side of the vehicle, then staggered towards his friend for cover.

'Clive!' he screamed.

'Get out of the way, Clive,' Ruth hissed in response. And as Blakely tried again to run for safety she fired a third shot that span him to the ground. Then, with every appearance of icy calm, Ruth Ellis came at her fallen lover and drilled two more bullets into his prone body. A sixth bullet ricocheted off the road to strike the thumb of a passing bank official's wife.

From the doorway of the pub, people were spilling out onto the street. An off-duty officer was among those present and he moved slowly towards her. 'Will you call the police?' Ruth asked softly as he took the gun. 'I *am* the police', he replied.

That, in bare outline, was the sequence of events that led Ruth Ellis to trial at the Old Bailey. In purely legal terms, it seemed a clear-cut case of wilful murder against which Ruth offered no substantial defence. She refused to ask for sympathy as a downtrodden mistress; in the dock she glossed over Blakely's beatings: 'He only used to hit me with his fists and hands, but I bruise very easily.' With all passion and anguish spent, Ruth Ellis *wanted* to die for the murder of her lover, and indulged in no tearful theatricals. To the disquiet of her lawyers, she even insisted on appearing in the dock with a full peroxide rinse. In the argot of the day she appeared the very archetype of a 'brassy tart'. Ruth's fate may have swung on that bottle of peroxide – with the chance injury to the bank official's wife's thumb.

In cross-examination, the prosecutor posed only one question:

'Mrs Ellis, when you fired that revolver at close range into the body of David Blakely, what did you intend to do?'

'It is obvious,' she replied with fateful simplicity, 'that when I shot him I intended to kill him.'

That, in effect, was that. The judge in summing up pointed out that jealousy was no defence under British law; the intention to kill was all-important. 'If, on the consideration of the whole evidence, you are satisfied that at the time she fired those shots she had the intention of killing or doing grievous bodily harm, then your duty is to find her guilty of wilful murder.'

Ruth herself had admitted her intention. The twelve members of the jury were out for only 23 minutes, and found the prisoner guilty of murder. Donning his black cap, the judge intoned the terrible words: 'The sentence of the Court upon you is that you be taken hence to a lawful prison, and thence to a place of execution, and that you there be hanged by the neck until you be dead . . .'

It all seemed so clear-cut. Yet, even under British law, it was not inevitable that Ruth Ellis should have hanged. Much about the case was never fully explored at the trial. Ruth's mental state, for example, was not discussed at any length: the effect of her second abortion, and the fact that she was taking tranquillisers on medical advice. The drugs, combined with alcohol she had consumed on the fateful day, may well have produced a state of serious psychological disturbance. Even on the given evidence, Blakely's violent provocations might have led the jury to recommend mercy. In the case of Kittie Byron (see page 10), such a recommendation had saved the prisoner from the gallows.

Then there was the question of the murder weapon. Ruth Ellis stated that she had been given the Smith and Wesson 'about three years ago by a man in a club whose name I don't remember.' Nobody believed this version of events even at the time. It was widely rumoured that Desmond Cussen had supplied the murder weapon, and also driven her to Hampstead on the fateful night. Interviewed in 1977, Cussen firmly repudiated the suggestions. The defence did not pursue the matter at the trial, since a hint of conspiracy to murder would have jeopardised the case for manslaughter, and the chance of a reprieve. Yet if someone did put the gun in Ruth's hand and drive her – befuddled with drink,

The notices of Ruth Ellis's execution are posted on the prison door

tranquillisers and lack of sleep – to the murder scene she would have been less easily presented as a cold-hearted blonde avenger.

During the last frenzied efforts to win Ruth a reprieve, this issue became electric. On the day before her execution, Ruth Ellis made a written statement to her solicitor Victor Mishcon:

> I, Ruth Ellis, have been advised by Mr Victor Mishcon to tell the whole truth in regard to the circumstances leading up to the killing of David Blakely and it is only with the greatest reluctance that I have decided to tell how it was that I got the gun with which I shot Blakely. I did not do so before because I felt that I was needlessly getting someone into possible trouble.
>
> I had been drinking Pernod (I think that is how it is spelt) in Cussen's flat and Cussen had been drinking too. This was about 8.30 p.m. We had been drinking for some time. I had been telling Cussen about Blakely's treatment of me. I was in a terribly depressed state. All I remember is that Cussen gave me a loaded gun . . . I was in such a dazed state that I cannot remember what was said. I rushed out as soon as he gave me the gun. He stayed in the flat.
>
> I had never seen the gun before. The only gun I had ever seen there was a small air pistol used as a game with a target.

Before signing the document, Ruth added:

> There's one more thing. You had better know the whole truth. I rushed back after a second or so and said 'Will you drive me to Hampstead?' He did so, and left me at the top of Tanza Road.

One view of this is that Ruth Ellis had no interest in saving her life at that stage, and was only persuaded to make her statement so that her ten-year-old son should know the truth. Desmond Cussen, however, in the 1977 interview, reiterated his claim to know nothing about the revolver, adding: 'She was a dreadful liar, you know.'

With only a few hours to spare, the statement was rushed by messenger to the Home Office. Scotland Yard was notified and Fleet Street buzzed with the news. Cussen, however, could not be found to comment on the statement and lacking a confession from him, the Home Secretary refused to consider the most urgent representations.

No reprieve was granted. Early in the morning of 13 July, Ruth Ellis wrote her last note to a friend from the condemned cell: 'The time is 7 o'clock a.m. – everyone (staff) is simply wonderful in Holloway. This is just to console my family with the thought that I did not change my way of thinking at the last moment. Or break my promise to David's mother.' That promise had been made in an earlier letter, in which Ruth had asked forgiveness and written, 'I shall die loving your son.'

And perhaps Ruth Ellis did die loving David Blakely. She spent her last hour in the death cell at prayer before a crucifix. Just before 09.00, the grim procession of officials entered and told her the time had come. They offered her a large measure of brandy which she gratefully accepted. Then, having thanked the authorities for their kindness, she walked steadily to the execution chamber where Albert Pierrepoint was waiting.

Chapter
Two

The Maddened Male

'Jealousy is cruel as the grave,' proclaims the biblical *Song of Solomon*. And since the dawn of time the malign spectre has haunted the precincts of love. Suspicion caused Dr Buck Ruxton to murder his blameless 'wife'; Elliot Bower to slay his best friend. At New York in 1906, a sensational drama of love and revenge was played out at Madison Garden's roof theatre. All were crimes committed by jealous husbands in the white heat of passion.

Yet a primitive belief attaches to the spectre of jealousy. By ancient tradition, when love is betrayed, vengeance is an honourable course. Two of Henry VIII's wives were found guilty of adultery and went to the block for high treason. Often, at lower levels of society, the maddened male may not see himself as a murderer at all – but as an executioner.

Murder on the Opening Night

It wasn't a very good show. Some of the biggest names in New York high society had turned up to see the new musical comedy opening on the roof garden of Madison Square Garden. *Mam'zelle Champagne* the entertainment was billed as, but its bubbles were flat and the fashionable socialites were yawning when the male lead got up to sing about love.

Then there was a gunshot; and another two shots. The orchestra stopped playing. And nobody yawned any more.

Harry Kendall Thaw, 34-year-old son of a Pittsburgh railroad magnate, was standing among the café-concert tables with a pistol smoking in his hand. Before him, Stanford White, the nation's most celebrated architect, was crumpled in his chair. Slowly he slid to the floor, blood spilling in crimson cataracts over his expensive shirt front. There were two bullet holes in his body. The third shot was lodged in his brain.

All around, people screamed and stampeded for the exits; vainly the manager called for the show to go on. The date was 25 June 1906, and the roof garden murder was to keep America reeling for months to come.

The public learned quickly that it was a love triangle killing. Thaw had publicly gunned down the seducer of his wife. 'I am glad I killed him. He ruined my wife', he had called on the fateful evening. But in this particular triangle were caught lurid shapes – of lust, sadism and madness – all refracted in the prism of big money.

The woman in the case was Evelyn Nesbit Thaw, the beautiful wife of the arrested gunman. Standards of prettiness change with the decades, but her beauty stands somehow outside time. The photographs show a pale, oval face, dark eyes, sensual mouth and lustrous curls. Frail and voluptuous, her features might have embodied the feminine mystique in a painting of any era.

In fact, Evelyn Nesbit had started out as an artist's model. But she soon moved on into the show world. At the age of 15 she was already appearing as a chorus girl in *Floradora*, a smash musical of the period. From the show one song is still well remembered: *Tell Me Pretty Maiden (Are There Any More at Home Like You?)* And from the high-kicking chorus line came another pretty maiden who appears in the pages of this book: Nan Patterson (see page 151).

Evelyn Nesbit had known the murdered architect long before she had known her husband. Stanford White was internationally respected for his building

Harry K Thaw dines in style behind bars

Stanford White

designs which included, ironically, Madison Square Garden itself. He was a large man with a florid complexion, moustachioed face and roué's lifestyle. On his first meeting with Evelyn he took her and another girl upstairs to a luxurious room in his apartment. It was equipped with a red velvet swing, and he gave the girls turns on it, pushing them right up to the ceiling where their feet reached a Japanese umbrella. But beyond his exotic décor and his playful games, White exhibited deeper passions. In his studio at the apartment, he soon had Evelyn posing for photographs in a silken kimono. On a later occasion, having dizzied her with champagne, he took her to a room whose walls and ceiling were covered with mirrors. There he seduced her while she was sleeping. She was still only 16 years old.

Evelyn went on to become one among several mistresses kept by the architect. He paid her weekly sums of money, brought her out into society and showed her off. Being married, to a very long-suffering wife, White could not offer the girl his hand. And that was one advantage which Harry K. Thaw had over the middle-aged architect.

Thaw met Evelyn Nesbit while she was going around with her seducer. And in the murder trial which was to come, his lawyers did what they could to suggest that Thaw had chivalrously redeemed the fallen showgirl. Certainly, Thaw was outraged by the story of the girl's initial seduction. He hated the architect, always referring to him as 'The Beast' and 'The Bastard'. But Thaw himself was no noble knight errant. Actually, he was a monster.

The spoiled playboy son of a millionaire family, Harry Thaw promised to marry Evelyn if she would run away with him to Europe. She accepted the offer, little knowing her admirer's sexual tastes. It was in the Tyrolean castle of Schloss Katzenstein that they were first revealed. One morning at breakfast in the rented castle, he stripped her of her bathrobe and left her naked except for her slippers. Producing a cowhide whip, he threw her onto the bed. 'I was powerless and attempted to scream,' the girl was to testify, 'but Thaw placed his fingers in my mouth and tried to choke me. He then, without any provocation, and without the slightest reason, began to inflict on me several severe and violent blows with the cowhide whip.'

She was in bed for three weeks afterwards, and other similar episodes were to occur before the marriage. It was one of Thaw's kinks, like the cocaine habit he had acquired. Other girls had received the same treatment at his hand.

Why did the chorus girl marry a man with such malevolent passions? Part of the answer must lie in the lure of the Thaw millions, amassed in railroads, coal and coke. There is evidence that some pressure was applied on Evelyn by her own family, and it is not hard to imagine their promptings: darling, your good looks won't last forever . . .

Stanford White could scarcely offer protection. In fact, he seems to have collaborated with her family in pressing for the marriage to go ahead. Whatever the reason, Evelyn Nesbit married Harry Thaw on 4 April 1905. It was a big society wedding in which the bride wore white despite the fact that the pair were known to have cohabited in New York already. The couple set up home in the Thaws' Pittsburgh mansion, and if the playboy's own family were none too happy about the marriage they made the best of it that they could.

It was Harry Thaw who became more and more unbalanced. He bought a pistol and was seen posing with it like a duellist in his bedroom. On 25 June, 1906, just over a year after his wedding, he took Evelyn to New York where they dined together at the Café Martin before going with friends to Madison Square Garden for the opening of *Mam'zelle Champagne*. Stanford White arrived later, and took a table on his own. The lacklustre performance had been going on for some time before Evelyn decided it was too dull to endure. The party rose, heading for the elevator. Evelyn in fact reached the lobby before noticing that her husband was not with the party.

Disarmed in the elevator moments after the shooting, Thaw was to explain to the District Attorney: 'I saw him sitting there, big, fat and healthy, and there Evelyn was, poor delicate little thing, all trembling and nervous.'

So spoke the sadist. The Thaw family was to spend hundreds of thousands of dollars not only on their son's legal defence, but on press campaigns to smear his victim. White, of course, presented an easy target for slander considering his roué's lifestyle. But Harry Thaw made no promising defendant either. His first trial for murder opened in January 1907 and did not end until some four months later. The jury eventually arrived at a split verdict. Seven declared Thaw guilty of first degree murder, but five held out for not guilty – by reason of insanity.

A year later, at a second trial, more was made of the issue of madness. Cases of mental disorder in the Thaw family were discussed; a brothel keeper described savage whippings that the defendant had administered to young girls. The jury on this occasion achieved a unanimous verdict. After 27 hours they voted Harry Thaw to be not guilty by reason of insanity.

Thaw was committed to the New York State Asylum for the Criminally Insane. And the story might have ended there but for the wealth and energy of his family who pressed continually for his release. Thaw did in fact taste freedom in 1913 – but not through any court decision. One morning in August he escaped the asylum, climbed into a waiting car and fled for sanctuary to Canada.

Much diplomatic pressure was exerted by the United States Government, and the fugitive was forced to return after only a month. He was jailed at Concord, New Hampshire, and eventually sent back to New York. Tirelessly, the Thaw family campaigned through their lawyers for his release. And in the end they won. In July 1915, as a result of yet another trial, Harry K. Thaw was declared both sane, and innocent of charges against him.

It was an extraordinary decision. Evelyn immediately divorced him and went off to live her own life. A free man, Harry Thaw responded to his good fortune only a few months later by kidnapping and cruelly horsewhipping a Kansas City youth who had incurred his displeasure. Again declared insane, he was again committed to an asylum. Again a court found him to be sane after all – and again, in 1924, he was released from custody.

Harry Thaw died of a coronary in Florida in February 1947. His case had made New York a Babel of gossip, loud rumour and frank accusation. But you do not have to be especially cynical to believe that, in the end, the most persuasive voice of all was the voice of money.

Harry and Evelyn Nesbit Thaw during a period of reconciliation

Suspicion

When Pauline Grandjean, a young dressmaker, became engaged to a man named Drouant she confessed a secret to her fiancé. The name she used, she said, was not her real one. There were good reasons for adopting the alias, but she was not prepared to divulge them.

Drouant accepted the arrangement, but he harboured his own suspicions. And when, one day in June 1905, he called unexpectedly at the girl's flat, those suspicions appeared fully confirmed. In her apartment was a postcard which bore the words: 'I shall come and see you this morning. You have my love in spite of all that has happened, and we will try and forget the past.'

His pulse quickening with jealous rage, Drouant concealed himself in the flat and awaited the arrival of the postcard's author. An hour or two later Pauline returned. She was followed almost immediately by a man who, on seeing her, fell into her arms.

Drouant sprang from his hiding place, forced the loving couple apart and plunged a knife deep into the man's back. The victim fell to the floor, his life ebbing with the blood that gushed from the wound.

'Murderer!' screamed the girl. 'You have killed my brother!'

It was a tragic episode which might have come straight from one of the stage melodramas of the period. The girl's brother had just served two years in prison and the pair had changed their names to avoid the stigma of his criminal record. He had written the card on the day of his release, intending to visit his sister briefly before going out to look for a job in Paris.

The victim was taken to hospital in his death throes. He refused to lay charges against his aggressor.

Chiller

An appalling crime of passion was reported from Paris in the Times in 1981. A Japanese student there shot his Dutch girlfriend dead because she refused to make love with him. Issei Sagawa, aged 32, then dismembered the body, putting parts in the refrigerator. These he subsequently ate.

The crime was discovered when the remainder of the body was found cut up and stuffed into two suitcases in the Bois de Boulogne. Mr Sagawa told police he had always wanted to eat a young woman.

Murder by our Paris Correspondent

How intrepid journalists are in detailing crimes of passion – how fearless in exposing lust and violence. These qualities were turned in on the profession by the great Morton-Bower scandal of 1852. The drama unfolded in Paris, and its male leads were both foreign correspondents.

Representing the *Morning Advertiser* was Mr Elliot Bower, aged forty and a bit of a wag. His friends knew him as a capital fellow much given to practical jokes. Once, for example, Bower crept up behind a blameless old gentleman who was studying the menu at an outside café table. The prankster suddenly grabbed him by the neck collar and the seat of his trousers and ran him along the boulevard. My, how they roared!

Representing the *Daily News* was Mr Saville Morton, elegant young man-about-town. Wealthy and much travelled, Morton was well known in the literary circles of the day. He was an intimate of Thackeray among other eminent writers, and became a foreign correspondent more for amusement than anything else. He did not need the money.

Both were Cambridge men who had been undergraduates together. And since they shared broadly the same liberal views, they worked closely together in Paris: swapping political gossip and sharing their insights into the latest intrigue. Morton was a bachelor, but Bower had married a Fanny Vickery in 1842. As chance would have it, Morton had known his friend's wife in London before the marriage. All seemed to conspire to cement the bonds of friendship, and the trio became boon companions who went to theatres and dined out constantly together. Sadly, it was not very long before the trio became a triangle.

Bower came to detect a threatening intimacy developing between his wife and his bachelor friend. At one stage there was a bitter quarrel, and Morton stopped visiting the Bowers' home in the rue de Sèze. The dispute was patched up, but it left an aura of mistrust which perhaps never entirely evaporated.

Elliot Bower, the jealous husband, was by no means irreproachable as far as the opposite sex was concerned. It must be remembered that the Paris of the day had a diamanté sparkle all of its own. This was the golden age of the *cocotte* and courtesan, of champagne and of *soupers intimes*. For the idling Englishman, the whole city glittered with temptation. And who could blame Mr Bower if, once in a while, he succumbed?

Mrs Bower could. The couple quarrelled frequently over Elliot's philandering ways. Some episodes sprang only from his prankster temperament: once, for example, he strolled up to a carriage in the Bois de Boulogne where a lady was seated in her carriage. Elliot thrust his hand through the window and squeezed her knee. As she gaped in astonishment, he made an elaborate bow and sped off in a waiting cab.

But there were more serious misdemeanours: candlelit suppers with *demi-mondaines* from which he came back late to the rue de Sèze. And things came to a head when Mrs Bower discovered that Elliot had been having an affair with an Englishwoman. Her name was Isabella Laurie, and Fanny found a letter from her husband's paramour, in which Isabella complained of having been seduced by Elliot and then cruelly cast aside.

Enraged, Mrs Bower turned to Saville Morton for comfort. Precisely what form that comfort took remains an issue in dispute. Certainly Mrs Bower wanted revenge against her husband, and was more than a little fond of Morton. The bachelor himself suggested a divorce and declared that he would marry her if she broke with her husband. Mrs Bower, however, demurred. It was not that she was unwilling, but the timing was awkward. The trouble was, she was expecting a baby.

It was in fact to be her fifth child. In due course, the baby was born with its mother still seething with rage. Two days after the event she had a message smuggled out via the concierge's wife: 'Go at once to Mr Morton, and tell him from me that the child is just like him.'

It all depends on how you interpret the case. Morton's reported reaction was, 'Goddam! Oh, what a nuisance.' This strongly implies that they had had an adulterous liaison which now threatened to be exposed. But if their love had never been consummated, it is possible to speculate that Morton thought the woman had become seriously unbalanced.

Whatever the truth, Morton kept a low profile *vis-à-vis* the Bowers for a fortnight after the birth. The issue was forced when Mrs Bower developed a fever and, tossing and turning in her delirium, kept calling out Morton's name. Despite her husband's objections, the bachelor was called for by the doctors to see if his presence would calm her. It did – and he stayed for several days and nights. The patient would only take medicine from Morton, who was put up in an adjoining room.

While the fever raged within her, Mrs Bower repeatedly insisted that her husband be kept away from her. Only once did she call him to her room. That was on the evening of 1 October 1852, and she took the opportunity to shriek imprecations against his infidelities. The tirade ended with the patient pointing to her sleeping child, and the words: 'Listen to me, you villain. That is not your child. Saville Morton, and not you, is its father. Oh, Queen of England, come to my help and rid me of this scoundrel!'

THE MADDENED MALE

How was Queen Victoria to intercede? Bower thought that his wife had gone mad and remained dutifully at her bedside. But she persisted. She referred to a particular period when he was in London . . . she had spent a night then with Mr Morton.

Bower tensed. Suddenly, he rushed from the room and confronted Morton with the charge. Morton failed to reply, promptly making for the stairs instead. Bower grabbed a carving knife and hurried after him, brandishing the blade. With one lunge he gashed the bachelor with a wound that severed Morton's carotid artery. The blood spilled everywhere.

Panic-stricken servants had witnessed the whole affair, and it was Bower who told them to send for a doctor. In the confused comings and goings which followed the assault, he in fact showed remarkable composure. Bower did not wait for the police or the medical assistance to arrive. Instead, he changed clothes, grabbed a passport and made for the Gare du Nord. A train took him to Boulogne; a packet-boat to England and safety.

News crossed frontiers in 1852 that policemen seldom did. The Morton-Bower affair soon had newspaper readers enthralled on both sides of the Channel. But though Morton died as a result of his wounds, Bower remained at liberty. He strolled the London streets in perfect freedom without the need for disguise or alias. The French police did contact Scotland Yard, but they made no request for the fugitive's arrest. And lacking this formal requirement, the London police were in no position to act. Incredibly, Elliot Bower even gave his own account of the Morton-Bower case for the *Morning Advertiser*. It was a more accurate piece than many which had been published about the sensation, a unique exclusive, really: Murder by Our Special Correspondent, as it were.

What of Mrs Bower? She had been committed to a lunatic asylum shortly after the fateful event. But she did not take long to recover (there was doubt as to whether she needed treatment at all). And before long she too had returned to London. She did not meet Bower there though; Fanny would have nothing to do with her husband, and expressed complete indifference as to his fate.

What that fate was to be remained problematic. Though the French made no move to extradite the fugitive, they did set the official legal machinery in action. After police investigations, a *juge d'instruction* (examining magistrate) determined that the crime was not murder but homicide. This heartened Bower. And knowing French lenience towards jealous husbands in a *crime passionnel*, it also encouraged him to make a bold move. Of his own free will, Elliot Bower returned to France and surrendered himself to the authorities.

The Assize Court in Paris was packed on 28 December as the Englishman faced his accusers. Bower entered the dock dressed in sober black, and his general demeanour was widely admired by the women in the courtroom. Not, however, by the *Gazette des Tribunaux*, which noted that the accused was 'a man

---

Springheeled Husband Pounced On Lovers

An irate husband flew into action on a homemade catapult when he saw his wife being cuddled by another man. He made a springboard out of a long plank and two car tyres and after a run launched himself into the air. He crashed head-first through the kitchen window of the house where his wife was being cuddled.

Mr Michael Garratt, prosecuting, told Dudley, Worcestershire, Crown Court that the husband landed in the sink and gently slid to the floor.

Graham Street, 21, of Rowley Regis, near Dudley, pleaded guilty to causing £1.49 damage to the window at the house on the Old Park Farm Estate at Dudley. He was put on probation for two years by Judge W.R. Davison and told not to 'indulge' in such 'amateur dramatics' again.

Mr John West, defending, said that the only person to get hurt was Street. He had no intention of interfering with his wife again.

Daily Telegraph

---

of between 35 and 40 years of age, blond, like most Englishmen, with luxuriant whiskers and an unfashionable moustache.'

The trial that followed in no way resembled the trials known to phlegmatic Anglo-Saxons. Take the supposedly neutral indictment, for example: this was one long torrent of abuse against the accused man, couched in terms of the most florid rhetoric. Describing, for example, Bower's philanderings it read: 'The villain flaunted his misconduct. And this in Paris! Oh, shame upon him!' Having luridly portrayed the assault on the unarmed Morton, it continued: 'What next? The murderer, blood on his hands and crime on his conscience, fled to England – to Perfidious Albion, where assassins are sheltered from outraged justice . . .'

All this before the prosecution began! Very little, it seemed, could be said for perfidious Englishmen with their unfashionable moustaches. The prosecution was an essay in defamation of character, in which foul innuendo, rank calumny and steamy prose jostled to take pride of place. Nobody disputed the fact that Bower had killed his rival. The main thrust of the prosecution's case was that the crime had been premeditated: Morton had been somehow enticed to the apartment in a cunning plot matured for some time beforehand. An absurd thesis, it is true, but it carried some weight when delivered with all the glowering malevolence that a Latin prosecutor can muster. Even Bower's voluntary surrender was scorned: a Frenchman would have done the honourable thing and given himself up on the spot. What did Bower do? He fled. Fled like an Englishman and now came brazenly back to cock a snook at the majesty of French law.

'I demand death for the murderer Bower!' roared the prosecutor at the end of his vehement declamation.

Even Bower, a cool enough customer, must have trembled inwardly as the dread words rang out. But help was at hand in the shape of a defence counsel equally armed with Gallic passion. He described the dastardly seduction of a previously chaste wife by a man thought to be a friend. He dwelled on the furtive liaison which developed, the passing of notes and so on. Bower's counsel had witnesses who confirmed that, on at least one occasion, Morton had spent a night with Mrs Bower when her husband was in London. And all the time the trusting and hard-working husband had been innocent of his betrayal!

The crime, declared the defence, was Morton's, not Bower's: 'What man among you, what husband and father worthy of the name would have acted otherwise? I tell you, gentlemen, the blow struck did him honour. The wife of his bosom had been seduced, her person possessed by another; and, as a result, adulterous offspring had been foisted upon him . . .'

The public in the court hissed and cheered at appropriate points. There was even one moment when, overcome by his own portrayal of the outraged husband's plight, the defence counsel actually broke down and wept piteously into a large handkerchief; the judge himself was so moved that the proceedings had to be halted for a while.

Then came the finale. The defence ended with a stirring appeal to those patriotic emotions which the prosecutor had tried to whip up.

'Remember that the accused has voluntarily surrendered to our courts, demanding justice at your hands. He has done well. French justice will not fail him. He will, by your verdict, go back to England and tell his countrymen there of the religious attention with which a French jury listens to the evidence, and that our French justice is everywhere the admiration of the world!'

Wild cheers! In no time at all, the jury declared for acquittal. The crowd roared its approval – strangers surged forward to wring Bower by the hand – the gendarmes even kissed him. It was as if the Englishman had been given the freedom of the city.

Bower did not, in fact, go back to England to celebrate French justice and French juries. On the contrary, Paris itself suited him very nicely. He lived there happily for the next 30 years, dying, aged 70, in 1884.

Wild Bill and his Women

In the old West, where female company was scarce, jealousy probably motivated more murders than cattle or bullion ever did. From bar-room brawls to main street showdowns the quarrels flared. Life was cheap, and many a legendary lawman owed notches on his gun not to zeal for the law – but to love of women.

Take Wild Bill Hickock, for example. The famed Union scout and Indian-fighter used to boast of a great Rock Creek shoot-out that began his crime-fighting career. The pistoleer claimed to have slain the ten-man McCanles gang single-handed: six bullets saw off Dave McCanles and five henchmen; he used a knife to cut down the other four villains. The West was well rid of the gang, said Hickock, for they were 'desperadoes, horse-thieves and murderers' to a man.

Wild Bill, of course, was one of the Wild West's great self-advertisers. Six foot two inches tall (wearing high-heeled shoes), with auburn curls that cascaded to his shoulders, the 'Prince of Pistoleers' made such an impressive figure that dude reporters from the East lapped up every word he said. In reality, James Butler Hickock was a drunk, a liar and a womanizer. As it happens, there was a McCanles episode – but it was not quite as Wild Bill told it.

In 1862, Hickock was working as a humble stable hand at the Rock Creek pony express station in Jefferson County, Nebraska. The manager there was a Mr Horace Wellman, and the stockkeeper a J.W. Brink. And in the offing, too, was a certain Sarah Shull (Kate Shell), something of a local belle.

Hickock stole the lady's affections from David C. McCanles, a landowner of the neighbourhood. And on 21 July 1862, the jealous McCanles rode out to the station threatening to 'clean up on the people' there. He was clearly intending a Wild-West style crime of passion, but had no cohort of desperadoes with him: just two neighbours and his 12-year-old son.

When the smoke cleared at Rock Creek that day, only the boy returned.

Years after the event, historical investigators succeeded in tracing the boy, Monroe McCanles. And he gave an account of the affair which reflected no credit on the legendary lawman. Monroe stated that when his father entered the station manager's house, Hickock shot him in the back with a rifle from a hidden position behind a curtain. Then Wild Bill turned the weapon on one of the neighbours, but only succeeded in wounding him; the man was beaten to death by Wellman who used a hoe. McCanles's second companion fled out into the scrub and was killed with a shotgun – Monroe could not say by whom.

So much for the solo slaying of ten desperadoes. Monroe's version of events

Wild Bill Hickock

was broadly confirmed in 1927, when investigators dug up court records from Nebraska. It appears that three men – Hickock, Wellman and Brink – were charged with the triple murder. The accused escaped punishment, however, on a plea of self-defence.

And did Wild Bill ride off into the sunset with the lovely Sarah Shull? Not a bit of it. He had a succession of paramours, and in 1865, his liaison with a certain Susanna Moore was to lead to the first Wild West showdown on record. A man named Dave Tutt took up with the lady and incurred the pistoleer's jealous wrath. A disputed card game provided Wild Bill with his pretext, and he challenged his rival to a gun duel in the public square at Springfield, Missouri.

The duel is an age-old means of settling a love-triangle quarrel: a kind of ritualised crime of passion. This one differed only from earlier gun duels in that the weapons were holstered. Tutt drew first, and missed. Before he had time to fire again, Hickock had put a bullet through his heart.

Off With Her Head!

Kings of the past possessed weapons of revenge unavailable to humbler citizens. A queen who took lovers threatened the royal succession. Adultery was treason, and two of Henry VIII's wives went to the block for the offence. The cases of Anne Boleyn and Catherine Howard were very different, but you could call each execution a judicial crime of passion.

Anne Boleyn was not, in conventional terms, an especially attractive woman. A contemporary described her as having a 'middling stature, swarthy complexion, long neck, wide mouth, bosom not much raised.' In fact, the observer declared, the Wiltshire girl had little to recommend her except for the king's appetite, 'and her eyes, which are black and beautiful and take great effect.'

Perhaps those dark eyes first drew Henry to her. Certainly, he wrote her some passionate love letters which have survived as evidence of real infatuation. Henry had his first marriage to Catherine of Aragon annulled in order to marry the English Anne. And though the first queen's failure to bear a male heir was a key reason for the divorce, Henry's love for Anne clearly strengthened his resolve.

When the pope refused to accept the divorce it sparked the immense upheaval of the English Reformation. And as for Henry and Anne, secretly married in January 1533, their union was not a success. The king's ardour soon cooled after the marriage and his eye started roving again. Anne bore him a daughter (the future Elizabeth I) instead of the son he desired. A second child miscarried and a third – a male heir – was dead at birth.

The stillborn child was delivered on 29 January 1536. And the unhappy event seems to have set the wheels of vengeance moving, for on 2 May, Anne Boleyn was sent to the Tower charged with adultery.

Four young courtiers were cited as her lovers: Sir Francis Weston, Henry Norris, William Brereton and Mark Smeaton. The most sensational charge, however, was that Anne had had carnal relations with her own brother, Lord Rochford; an accusation instigated by his spiteful wife. All except Smeaton protested their innocence, the latter confessing to guilt. All went to the block, Smeaton declaring on the scaffold that he 'deserved to die'.

Anne for her part persistently professed herself innocent. When she heard of Smeaton's last words she erupted with passion: 'Has he not cleared me of that public shame he has brought me to? Alas, I fear his soul suffers for it and that he is now punished for his false accusation.' She was tried and unanimously

King Henry VIII

Anne Boleyn

condemned by a court of 30 peers. The sentence carried with it an option for Henry – she could be either burnt alive or beheaded, according to the king's pleasure.

Henry, bountiful in her mercy, opted for beheading. He even had an especially sharp blade imported from the Continent for, as the queen observed with sad vanity: 'I have but a little neck.'

Anne went to the scaffold on 19 May, behaving with courage and dignity. It was said that she had never appeared more beautiful than on that fateful day. Still professing her innocence, she graciously declared that the king had done her many favours: first in making her a marchioness, second in making her a queen, third in sending her to heaven.

It is easy to imagine her a tragic victim of circumstance. Nevertheless, her own uncle presided over the court of peers which found her guilty. They saw evidence which was subsequently destroyed. And no-one, not even her own daughter Elizabeth, later tried to retrieve her reputation. Smeaton's confession, her friends' silence, the peers' unanimous judgement – all tend to suggest that she may well have been an unfaithful wife.

Still, callous statecraft clearly played its part in the affair. The king craved a male heir and did not mourn his second wife's passing. He was seen immediately after the execution wearing bright yellow garb with a feather in his cap. And the very next day he became betrothed to Jane Seymour, his third wife. She was to die not long after giving birth to the boy child he so desperately desired (the sickly Edward VI). The fourth wife, Anne of Cleves, lasted no time at all. Henry only married her to effect a German alliance, and found her so ugly on sight that he divorced her immediately. It was then that the ill-starred Catherine Howard came into his life.

Catherine was the orphaned daughter of a noble and gallant soldier, and was brought up in the household of her grandmother, Agnes, Duchess of Norfolk. The girl was pretty, young and vivacious and Henry, now 50, fell passionately in love with her. He called her his 'rose without a thorn,' and she seemed to come fresh with all the innocence of virginal maidenhood.

Unfortunately for all concerned, this was an illusion.

Catherine had committed many youthful indiscretions. And almost immediately after the wedding in July 1540, these came to the attention of the king's councillors. A former maidservant in the Duchess of Norfolk's household had confided to her brother Catherine's misconduct. The brother in turn approached Archbishop Cranmer. The queen, it appeared, had not been a virgin when she married, and the maidservant's story was as picturesque as it was disquieting:

'Marry, there is one Francis Dereham who was servant also in my Lady Norfolk's house which hath been in bed with her in his doublet and hose

Anne Boleyn being sentenced

between the sheets an hundred nights. And there hath been such puffing and blowing between them that once in the house a maid which lay in the house with her said to me she would lie no longer with her for she knew not what matrimony meant.'

Nor was it just Dereham who had dallied with the English rose. A man named Mannock 'knew a privy mark of her body.'

This was an awkward business. Cranmer himself had arranged the marriage and his reputation was at stake. He is said to have been 'marvellously perplexed' as to what to do about the report and called two other high officials of state who were equally troubled. Cranmer, they decided, really must inform the king, even if the story was just malicious gossip. The Archbishop agreed, but dared not face his sovereign in person. Instead he submitted a written report and waited for the storm to break.

Henry was outraged. He refused to believe it. He questioned Catherine about the allegations, and she was fierce in her denials. And though Henry desperately wanted to believe her, his obligations required that he secretly assemble a group of notables to investigate the allegations. Dereham and Mannock, the maidservant and her brother, were all tracked down and closely questioned. And when the various reports came back, the picture looked very dark for Catherine.

Henry Mannock, for example, turned out to be a musician who admitted that he 'commonly used to feel the secrets and other parts of her body.' Francis Dereham seemed once to have been betrothed to Catherine, and confessed that he had known her carnally 'many times both in his doublet and hose and in naked bed.' He also named three young ladies who had joined with them in the bedroom athletics. And he said that Thomas Culpepper, Catherine's own cousin, was another of her lovers.

Henry VIII – bold scourge of the pope and the monasteries – wept like a baby when he heard the news. For some time he was so overcome with emotion that words failed him entirely. He loved his English rose and still refused to credit the stories. But he was like a man trying to cross a muddy field in gumboots. With every step he took, the mire went on loading his feet.

As investigations proceeded, it became clear that practically the whole household of the Duchess of Norfolk had conspired to keep up a pretence of Catherine's chastity. Lady Jane Rochford (the spiteful wife of Anne Boleyn's executed brother) was reported to have encouraged Catherine's youthful frolics. She too was arrested and questioned – and was to go to the block in due course.

Bitterly galling all this must have been to the deceived monarch. But so far, the allegations all concerned Catherine's behaviour before the marriage. There was worse – much worse to come. Henry discovered that after the wedding,

Catherine had appointed the lusty Dereham to a post in her royal household. He had been writing some of the Queen's letters for her – they had been alone together in her bedchamber without the presence of servants or other members of the household.

Adulteress! The spell of the king's disbelief was broken and he had Catherine formally arrested. When questioned, she persisted in her denials until confronted with the haul of confessions from miscellaneous lovers and servants. Faced with their frank statements, she broke down and admitted her youthful unchastity to the Archbishop. She still maintained, however, that she had been faithful as a wife.

The queen's confession was enough to seal the fates of the leading men in the case. Culpepper, a man of noble birth, was beheaded. Dereham and Mannock, both lowlier paramours, were hanged and quartered. Assorted members of the Howard family and household were arrested on the charge of misprision of treason – that is to say, concealing their knowledge of an intention to deceive the king.

Poor, wretched Catherine was now charged with adultery. But still the anguished king and his distressed councillors were reluctant to act decisively. The Lord Chancellor, for example, asked the Lords for a delay in the trial proceedings. The queen, he said, must be given a chance to clear herself of the charge. The Lords willingly agreed to the proposal. But within a couple of days, the king's own Privy Councillors pressed for a speedy resolution. They did, however, add a clause which speaks volumes for Henry's miserable state of mind. The king, they declared, need not actually attend Parliament as it assessed the evidence; he need only sign the documents when judgement was passed. This unusual arrangement was suggested because the 'sorrowful story and wicked facts if repeated before him might renew his grief and endanger His Majesty's health.'

Henry agreed to the proposal, which must have been a great relief to the Lords. They would now be able to speak their minds freely without their impetuous sovereign glowering at them from behind his beard. As in the case of Anne Boleyn, the trial records were subsequently destroyed. But it appears that Catherine did confess to 'the great crime she had been guilty of against the most high God and a kind Prince and against the whole English nation.' She asked no mercy for herself, but only for the friends and relations who had been implicated with her.

Catherine Howard was beheaded on Tower Hill on 13 February 1542. We do not know how she faced her end. But we do know that the king took no more frisky nymphs to the altar. The following year he married the patient and motherly Catherine Parr – his 6th wife – who subsequently managed to outlive him.

The Headless Wife Case

It had all the ingredients of a Gothic horror story. They included the decomposing body of the beautiful wife – kisses delivered by her husband to the corpse – the severed head saved in remembrance. The story should have been set in some dark and sinister castle. But it wasn't. The drama unfolded in tranquil West Wycombe; it was a crime for the 1980s.

Michael Telling, 34, was a member of the vastly rich Vestey family behind the Dewhurst butchers' chain. His second cousin was Lord Vestey, multi-millionaire and polo-playing friend of royalty. In terms of material advantage, Telling enjoyed immense privileges. Being a beneficiary of the Vestey Trust, he received £1,200 a month pocket money – all his bills and credit card accounts were paid on top of that.

He could afford all the expensive toys he desired: fast cars, motorcycles, guns and stereo equipment. The Vestey millions paid for holidays all around the world. But they could not pay for the one thing that Telling needed. Money never did buy love.

He had had a miserable childhood. His father was an aggressive alcoholic who chased his pregnant mother brandishing swords. The mother herself was to testify that she had rejected her son. At an early age, Michael was packed off to boarding school and there, being a sickly boy, he was bullied mercilessly. When he reacted by stealing, starting fires and playing truant, he was beaten by the staff.

He became a problem child: emotionally disturbed and barely controllable in his actions. Twice expelled, he eventually went to a special school for maladjusted children, as well as becoming an inmate at a mental hospital. At home he was kept away from the family and raised by nannies and governesses. When only nine years old he was drinking sherry and smoking heavily. He kept carving knives in his room and once threatened his mother with a blade.

It was from this wrecked childhood that he entered adult life. In 1978, Michael Telling married his first wife, 18-year-old Alison, whom he had first met in Australia. The couple had a son, but the relationship was not to last. Telling was a 'coward who was unable to face his responsibilities,' she was to say. In 1980 he went to America to buy his latest toy, a Harley-Davidson motorcycle. While trying out his new machine at Sausalito near San Francisco, he pulled up at some traffic lights and fell into a conversation with a Mr and Mrs Zumsteg. They suggested that he meet their daughter, Monika.

Within three days of the encounter, he was sleeping with Monika. And shortly

67

after his return to England, he informed his wife that he had found another woman. In 1981, a divorce was arranged. Less than a month later, Michael Telling married Monika Zumsteg.

Much was said at the trial about his bride. Monika was headlined in one paper as a 'SEX MAD GOLD-DIGGER', and she certainly lived her life in the fast lane. Monika drove a Pontiac Firebird and drank Benedictine and orange for breakfast. She used cocaine, heroin and marijuana. In her handbag she carried a gun and a vibrator.

The couple lived at opulent Lambourn House, West Wycombe in Buckinghamshire. Luxury items included a whirlpool bath on the lawn where Monika would frolic with naked party guests. Her husband used to sit on the sidelines, drinking. She said he was only good for money. On frequent occasions, she publicly belittled his sexual efforts, boasting to him of her own lovers both male and female.

When the marriage came to its gruesome end, neighbours were to confirm the stories. Richard Richardson, for example, was an odd-job man and a friend of the Tellings. He said that Monika told him she had no intention of making a life with her husband and that 'all she wanted was his money.' Once, she told Richardson that, 'I could f . . . any man, any woman better than any man can. I am AC/DC. Man or woman – I go with anybody.' She seemed to take a vindictive pleasure out of humiliating her husband. Richardson had been present on one occasion when Monika had ordered Telling to make coffee, shouting, 'Get off your f . . . arse, you mother-f . . . Make the coffee!' Telling begged her not to talk like that and affectionately ran kisses up her arm. On another occasion, the couple had a play fight in the kitchen. Monika took the opportunity to knee Telling in the groin. 'He went white, but said nothing.'

'He worshipped the ground she walked on,' said Richardson, 'but she showed no affection. She said she would only stay with him for two years to get money out of him.' Telling had to visit his son secretly because Monika disapproved, saying that the boy was horrible and she hated him.

Telling's first wife, Alison, told much the same story. Once, Monika had visited her home, bringing a bottle of gin and a cockatoo. She smoked cannabis, drank Drambuie and took four or five pills. She complained to Alison that Michael was no good in bed, saying she did not want a divorce until she'd got some of his money. Monika said that she was prepared to get herself pregnant and go back to America with the baby to get the cash.

Telling himself was to refer to countless humiliations. Once, he had seen her frolicking half naked with another woman on the living-room floor. Yet on their honeymoon night at the Hyde Park Hotel in London, she refused to have sex with her husband. In fact, she banned sex entirely with Telling for the last seven months of her life.

Monika was doomed to become the Headless Wife. She never got a chance to defend herself against these allegations in court. But her father was to claim that the stories were outrageous: 'She was certainly not a saint, but she was nothing like she was painted. She was too flippant sometimes, like when she told a neighbour she was AC/DC. It's the kind of thing she would say for a laugh. Monika was a woman of great intelligence, kind and full of sensitivity.'

Whatever the truth, the relationship seems to have been founded on a disastrously flawed combination of personalities. She certainly liked fast living – he certainly needed love. And successive episodes illustrate how the marriage was heading for calamity. In 1982, Monika took up an Alcoholics Anonymous programme. Telling, meanwhile, underwent treatment in a psychiatric hospital. He was to claim that Monika tried to run him down with a car and attacked him with a whip. But he also admitted that he sometimes retaliated, and had attacked her on four occasions during their 17-month marriage.

The terrible climax came on 29 March 1983. By Telling's account, she was delivering a tirade in the living room, shouting that he ought to be sent to a mental hospital. The taunts finally shattered his eggshell personality. 'She came charging towards me. I thought she was going to attack me so I picked up the rifle and shot her.'

The weapon in question was a Marlin 30-30 hunting gun, and he shot her three times. She was hit in the throat and the chest. 'I kissed her then and said I was sorry. But I knew she was dead.'

If the case had ended there it would have been sensational enough. What happened next turned it into an almost unbelievable horror story. Telling left the body for two days where it was before carrying it into a bedroom: 'I went to look at her every day and kissed her often.' He also talked to the corpse as it lay on a camp bed. Eventually, he dragged the body to a summer house, a building half-converted into a sauna. And there it remained for five months.

Telling told his friends that Monika had left him to return to her native America. As 'protection' for himself, he installed an elaborate security system at his home, and even employed private detectives to find his wife.

During this period, as Monika's body lay decomposing at Lambourn House, Telling started to see a former friend called Mrs Lynda Blackstock. She spent three or four nights at his home, and he tried to woo her in his bedroom. But he could not make love successfully. 'He told me all about Monika', she was to say. 'He told me she was an alcoholic, a drug addict and a lesbian. Michael said she had gone back home to the U.S. – and he was glad.' At the trial, she was asked:

'There was not a hint that Monika lay dead in the very building you were visiting?'

Mrs Blackstock: 'Definitely not.'

Another recent girl friend, divorcée Mrs Susan Bright, also went to bed with

Telling after he had killed his wife. She slept with him several times and the couple went out for meals together. She said: 'He was very talkative, although he seemed very nervous . . . I asked him if he had heard from Monika at all and he said he thought she was in America.'

In September 1983, Telling hired a van and drove to Devon with the body. On Telegraph Hill outside Exeter he cut off Monika's head with an axe. He dumped the headless body there but could not bear to part with the head itself. Instead, he brought it home and hid it in the locked boot of his Mini in the garage. It was kept there wrapped in plastic.

Two days later, a Devon man stumbled on the headless body. Though badly decomposed by now, it still wore a distinctive Moroccan T-shirt. And although it had been decapitated, a chunk of hair and a few teeth were found at the site.

' The gruesome discovery made the national news, and Mrs Richardson's interest was alerted. She knew that Monika had a similar T-shirt, and was nonplussed when Telling confessed to her that he had killed his wife: 'She is in the sauna – it's stinking.'

Although Mrs Richardson did not believe him, she did eventually inform the police. At this stage, Monika was just one among many missing young women who vaguely fitted the description pieced together from the remains. But dental tests on the few teeth found revealed that the victim had suffered from a disorder of the gums. Monika, had recently undergone an operation for a gum infection.

Devon detectives went to the West Wycombe house and found the dead woman's skull in the Mini. Exactly a week after the body was discovered, Michael Telling was arrested.

He confessed the killing to the police. Asked why he had shot her he replied, 'There were 101 reasons. I can't really explain. She kept pushing me. I just snapped in the end. She was horrible in many ways.'

Horrible in many ways – the phrase might serve as an epitaph on the whole case. Asked why he had cut off her head, Telling replied, 'I did not want her identified because of my family. Even when she died I wanted her to be with me.'

The case was tried at Exeter Crown Court in June 1984. He pleaded not guilty to murder, but guilty to manslaughter by reason of diminished responsibility.

The press, of course, had a field day. 'MISTRESSES TELL OF SEX IN THE HOUSE OF HORROR' – 'SEX SESSIONS AS BODY LAY NEAR-BY', blared the headlines. The public learned that Telling had taken Mrs Bright out to a Chinese meal in High Wycombe just 24 hours after he had chopped off his wife's head.

If the press dwelled on the bizarre, macabre details, the courtroom wrangling revolved around Telling's state of mind. No-one denied that the defendant had killed his wife; he himself furnished most of the details. The question in dispute was whether he was responsible for his actions.

Michael and Monika Telling on their wedding day

THE WORLD'S GREATEST CRIMES OF PASSION

The prosecution pressed for a verdict of murder. It dwelt on the 'amazing catalogue' of gruesome lengths to which Telling went to avoid detection. He had told a psychiatrist that the seed of the crime was planted four days before the event. On the evening before the killing, the time and method were, allegedly, decided. 'Despite his mental abnormality, this man determined to kill his wife. He could have prevented himself from doing so if he wished.'

Afterwards, to conceal the crime, he used his wife's Cashpoint card until the account was almost depleted, so giving the impression that she was still alive. He hired the private detectives. He made an 'elaborate pretence' of going on a camping trip when he travelled to Devon to dump the body. As for the head, the prosecution alleged, he did not take it home for remembrance – but to avoid identification of the corpse.

Set against all this apparent cunning was the testimony of psychiatrists, friends and relations. The defence stressed the defendant's maimed and disordered personality. Telling's grey-haired mother appeared in the witness box and described how as a boy he had witnessed violent arguments between herself and his alcoholic father. She told how he would run naked into the road in front of traffic; how he twice attempted suicide. She acknowledged that her son was a boy deprived of affection: 'Many of Michael's problems stem from his very lonely and unhappy childhood.'

Telling wept in the dock as his mother gave evidence, and he delayed the hearing by 15 minutes after passing a note to his lawyers asking for an adjournment. The note was strangely worded and misspelt: 'You get Mum away from this awful trial, or I will get up and let the bloddy prosoqutor hear what I think off.'

He was visibly moved too when a former school companion entered the box 'out of a sense of guilt' after reading newspaper reports. The man, Bertram Lilley, described the vicious bullying that Telling had endured: before the boys would let him join in a game they made him roll in a patch of stinging nettles until he resembled 'one large blister'. Even then he could not play because he was too badly hurt.

Lilley's parents had lived in Africa at the time and he once spent a half-term at the Tellings. There was more love, he said, across the many miles to Africa 'than across the living room of that house.'

Telling was close to tears as the testimony was given. Otherwise he remained an enigma: slightly balding, dressed in Savile Row pinstripes and paying rapt attention to the trial. A psychiatrist described how Monika's sexual taunts and her ban on lovemaking would have been humiliating and distressing even to a normal man. But Telling was not normal; he did not know how to cope. His responsibility was 'substantially impaired' at the time of the killing.

The judge in summing up reminded the court that psychiatry is not an exact science. Ultimately, the jurors were as fit as anyone else to assess whether Telling was responsible for his actions. Yet they seem to have agreed with the psychiatrist. For after $2\frac{1}{2}$ hours deliberation, the jury found the defendant not guilty of murder but guilty of manslaughter on the grounds of diminished responsibility.

Gaoled for life, Michael Telling was to remain in custody until those responsible felt it 'safe and proper' to release him.

Edgar the Peaceful

'**T**he reign of Edgar was somewhat uneventful,' muses the *Encylopaedia Britannica*. King of a united England (959–975), this Anglo Saxon monarch was noted mainly for his church reforms and known as 'Edgar the Peaceful' in consequence.

Yet his personal life did not lack excitements. Aged 17, the king sired a child by a nun at the convent of Wilton; she refused to marry him. Then Edgar took his first wife, and not long afterwards heard glowing reports about a beautiful Lady Elfrida, daughter of Devonshire's Earl Ordgar. To find out if the stories were true he sent his servant Athelwold to look her over as a prospective second wife. Athelwold went and found that Elfrida was all that had been rumoured. He fell in love with her and, instead of reassuring his monarch, sent a dispatch that the girl was stupid and ugly and he married her himself.

Athelwood took his new bride to his estate in Hampshire, and dared not present her at court. The king wondered why she never made her appearance, and so did Elfrida herself. Then came a fateful day when the king came to hunt in nearby forests. He sent word that he would spend the night at Athelwold's estate.

The courtier was in a quandary. He could not refuse his sovereign, and so ordered his wife to dress 'in fowle garments, and some evil favoured attire' so that her beauty would be hidden. Elfrida, however, refused to comply and decked herself out in all her finery. When the king saw her he was smitten with her loveliness. He took her husband hunting with him in a wood, 'not showing that he meant anie hurt, till at length he had got him within the thicke of the wood, where he suddenly stroke him through with his dart.'

Having murdered the deceitful courtier, Edgar the Peaceful married Elfrida. She bore him two sons (one of whom was Ethelred the Unready) and the couple presided together over the remainder of his tranquil reign.

Bunkum With a Capital B

The most infamous doctors in the annals of crime were generally cunning poisoners. Dr Ruxton's case was different. It is true that he used his medical knowledge to a gruesome degree in trying to cover up his atrocity. But all the facts indicate that the murder itself was an impulse killing accomplished in a state of high emotion. No science or stealth contributed to the initial act – his was a crime of passion.

He was born in Bombay as Bukhtyar Rustamji Ratanji Hakim and qualified in his native country. Moving to England, he was made a Bachelor of Medicine in London. After further studies at Edinburgh he took up a practice in Lancaster in 1930. It was at about that time that he changed his name by deed poll to that of Dr Buck Ruxton.

With him to London came Isabella Van Ess, a married woman from Edinburgh. Her husband divorced her when she followed the doctor down. And although Isabella never married Dr Ruxton she lived with him as his wife. She also bore him three children, and was known to everyone simply as Mrs Ruxton.

They lived with the children at No. 2 Dalton Square, Lancaster. The doctor was highly regarded in his profession and well liked by all of his patients. This was despite the fact that the doctor and his 'wife' had an intensely emotional relationship. The couple quarrelled incessantly and often came to blows. But they always made up afterwards. At the trial, patients were to remember how Mrs Ruxton would rush into her husband's surgery and urgently embrace him to achieve a reconciliation.

The rows, though, were more than mere tiffs. Ruxton commonly threatened his wife and once held a knife to her throat. On two separate occasions the police were called in, but Mrs Ruxton never pressed charges. On the whole, she seems to have given as good as she got. 'We were the kind of people who could not live with each other and could not live without each other', the doctor was to admit.

Once, Mrs Ruxton attempted suicide to try and escape from the bonds that tied them together. And in 1934 she fled to her sister in Edinburgh intending a final breach. Ruxton, however, followed her and persuaded her to come back to him and to their children.

The root of the problem appears to have been Ruxton's obsessive jealousy. Constantly he accused his wife of infidelity, complaining on c᷈ ᷈occasion that she behaved like a common prostitute. His morbid suspicions were entirely without foundation, but jealousy feeds on chance happening and trifling coincidence. Things came to a head in autumn 1935, when Ruxton persuaded himself that she was having an affair with a young town clerk named Robert Edmondson.

On 7 September, the Edmondson family drove up to Edinburgh. Their party included Robert, his sister and parents. And they agreed to take Mrs Ruxton up too for a visit to her native city.

Seething with suspicion, Ruxton abandoned his surgery and followed them in a hired car. He discovered that his wife was staying in the same hotel as the family, rather than with her sister as planned. It was for a perfectly innocent reason, but back in Lancaster, Ruxton was to rant for days at his wife about her supposed liaison.

On 14 September, the following weekend, Mrs Ruxton made another blameless excursion. Taking the doctor's Hillman, she drove to Blackpool as she did once every year to see the illuminations with her sisters. She left the resort at 23.30 that night, intending to go back the next day. But she never did return to Blackpool. In fact, having driven back to Dalton Square in the car, she never went anywhere again. Not in one piece, that is.

It is known that she reached home, because Ruxton was using the Hillman the next day and in the period that followed. It is known too that the doctor was in the house with his three children and the housemaid, Mary Rogerson. The children were all under five; Mary Rogerson was aged 20. But she could give no account of what transpired that night, for Mary Rogerson disappeared with Mrs Ruxton. The next time anyone but the doctor saw the two women they were barely identifiable: no more than dismembered chunks of bone, tissue and skin all wrapped up in bloodsoaked packages.

The story emerged at the trial. It has to be assumed that Ruxton was waiting in a mood of frenzied suspicion. There was yet another row which this time reached its climax in bloody murder. Ruxton killed his wife with a sharp-bladed instrument, and Mary Rogerson no doubt saw everything. She had to die too – and afterwards began the grisly business of destroying the evidence.

From what is known of Ruxton's character, anguish, remorse – and concern for his children – must have been coursing through his veins. But he set to work like a Trojan on the bodies of the two women and the welter of blood everywhere. Probably he worked all night while the children slept, and still there was much to be done.

One of the family's three charladies, Mrs Oxley, was due to arrive at 07.00 on Sunday morning. At 06.30, as she was preparing to leave her home, Dr Ruxton appeared on her doorstep. It was the astonished Mr Oxley who opened the door, with his wife standing not far behind him. Both heard what Ruxton said quite clearly: 'Tell Mrs Oxley not to trouble to come down this morning. Mrs Ruxton and Mary have gone away on a holiday to Edinburgh and I am taking the children to Morecambe. But tell her to come tomorrow.'

The 'murder ravine' where the bundles of human remains were found

At the trial, Ruxton was to deny that he had ever been to the Oxleys' house.

Returning home, Ruxton made the children's breakfast. He received the Sunday papers and milk, delivery women noting that he seemed to be shielding an injured hand. On a brief excursion in the Hillman he bought a full tank of petrol and two spare gallons besides.

Nursing his wounded hand, Ruxton was busy all Sunday. A woman patient turned up at Dalton Square with a child needing treatment. Ruxton postponed the appointment, saying that he was busy taking up carpets because decorators were due the next morning. At midday, he asked a neighbour to look after his children for the afternoon, saying that his wife had gone with Mary to Scotland and that he had cut his hand opening a tin of fruit at breakfast.

That afternoon he toiled undisturbed at the house until it was in a more or less presentable state. Then, at 16.30, he called on a friend and patient, Mrs Hampshire, to ask if she would help him get the house ready for the decorators. It was in a strange condition when she arrived. The carpets on stairs and landing had been taken up, and straw was scattered around. It even bristled out from under the two main bedroom doors – which were locked and remained so all evening.

In one room was a bloodstained suit; in the backyard were bloodstained carpets. Ruxton asked if she would be kind enough to clean the bath. It was filthy, with a grubby yellow stain extending high around the inside of the tub.

At the trial, Ruxton was to claim that the blood marks all derived from the severely gashed wound to his hand. But there was an awful lot of it about and, daunted by the size of the task, Mrs Hampshire asked if she could get her husband to help. Ruxton agreed, and the business of cleaning up went on until 21.30. As a reward for their labours, Ruxton offered the pair the stained suit and carpets, which they took with them when they left.

Presumably, the bodies were in the two locked bedrooms. No doubt the doctor was not idle that night. And he must have had nagging fears about the stained articles he had given the Hampshires, for first thing on Monday morning he went round to their house and asked for the suit back. He stood there, dishevelled and unshaven, explaining that he wanted to send it to the cleaner's. Mrs Hampshire insisted that she was quite happy to take it for cleaning herself. Ruxton then demanded that she take the name-tag from it, claiming that it would be improper for her husband to go around wearing a suit with another man's name in it. She duly cut it off. 'Burn it now', he demanded, and she tossed the tag onto her fire.

Afterwards, she looked at the suit and found the waistcoat so badly stained that she also put that on the flames. As for the carpets, she was to testify: 'The amount of blood on the third carpet was terrible. It was still damp where the blood was, and it had not been out in the rain. I laid the carpet in the backyard and threw about 20 or 30 buckets of water on it to try to wash the blood off, and the colour of the water that came off was like blood. I threw it on the line and left it to dry, and when it was washday I had another go at it with the yard brush and water, and still could not get the congealed blood off.'

In the week that followed, the doctor kept fires going night and day in his own backyard. He called in the decorators. And when the charladies complained of peculiar smells about the house he replied by spraying Eau de Cologne around.

To neighbours, Ruxton gave varied and inconsistent accounts about why Mrs Ruxton and Mary were away. To one he confided, sobbing and agitated, that the pair had gone to London, where his wife had eloped with another man. But Mary's parents, the Rogersons, were not easily convinced. Eventually, Ruxton told them that their daughter had been got pregnant and that this accounted for her going away. Mr Rogerson was undeterred. He threatened to ask the police to find his daughter.

At some stage (probably Thursday 19 September) Ruxton must have driven up to Scotland. For ten days later, exactly two weeks after the women vanished, the first grisly package was discovered.

A woman found it by a bridge near Moffat, off the Carlisle-Edinburgh road. She saw what seemed to be a human arm protruding from a wrapped bundle at the water's edge. Horrified, she called her brother who in turn summoned the police. The constable found four bundles: 'a blouse containing two upper arms and four pieces of flesh; a pillowslip enclosing two arm bones, two thigh bones, two lower leg bones, and nine pieces of flesh; part of a cotton sheet containing 17 pieces of flesh; and another piece of sheet containing the chest portion of a human trunk and the lower portions of two legs.'

More parcels were to turn up in due course. The police determined that pieces from two separate bodies had been jumbled up in the packages together. But certain distinguishing characteristics had been removed: some of the teeth, eyes and finger ends (presumably to prevent fingerprint identification). In fact, during the early investigation, the surgical removal of various organs made it impossible to discover the sex of the victims. The police began by announcing that they believed the bodies to be those of a man and a woman.

Reading this news in his daily paper seems to have given Ruxton some rare moments of good humour. In jovial mood, he told one of the charladies, 'So you see, Mrs Oxley, it is a man and a woman, it is not our two.' On another occasion: 'Thank goodness the other one in the Moffat case was a man and not a woman' – or people would be saying that he had murdered his wife and Mary.

But the police had already connected the Moffat bodies with the doctor's home town. One of the bundles had been wrapped in a copy of the *Sunday Graphic* dated 15 September (the murder morning). It happened to be a special edition sold only in Morecambe and Lancaster.

On 9 October, the Rogersons reported their daughter a missing person. On that day too, Ruxton asked Mrs Hampshire what she had done about the suit: 'Do something about it', he insisted. 'Get it out of the way. Burn it!' On 14 October, the doctor was taken into custody and questioned at length. In the small hours of the next day he was charged with Mary's murder. Cautioned, he protested, 'Most emphatically not, of course not. The furthest thing from my mind. What motive and why? What are you talking?' Some days later he was also charged with the murder of his wife, and it was on this indictment that he was to stand trial at the Manchester Assizes.

Precisely identifying the two bodies remained problematic for the authorities. The affair was to become something of a textbook case in medico-criminal history. A team of pathologists and anatomists fitted together their grim jigsaw of remains, proving that the age and size of the missing women roughly matched those of Bodies I and II. But key features had been removed. For example, Mrs Ruxton had prominent teeth and these had been withdrawn. Miss Rogerson had a squint – the eyes had been taken from their sockets. Nevertheless, it did prove possible to identify Mary's body by fingerprints. And Mrs Ruxton was identified when a photograph superimposed on Head II matched exactly.

It was proved that the doctor had been delivered the local edition of the *Sunday Graphic* for 15 September. Moreover, the linen sheet in which one bundle was wrapped was the partner of a single sheet left on Mrs Ruxton's bed.

The doctor made a miserable impression in the witness box. He vehemently denied the testimony of his charladies and his neighbours, claiming for example that he never visited the Oxleys; that he never asked Mrs Hampshire to burn the suit. His own account of his movements was deeply implausible and his manner both pitiable and arrogant. Sometimes he sobbed and became hysterical; sometimes he waxed bombastic. Once, taxed with murdering his wife and disposing of the witness, he replied, 'That is absolute bunkum with a capital B'.

A fit verdict on his own hopeless attempts to clear himself. Ruxton was found guilty, and when an appeal failed he was hanged at Strangeways Prison. The date was 12 May 1936. Soon afterwards, his own terse confession was published, a note penned at the time of his arrest,

I killed Mrs Ruxton in a fit of temper because
I thought she had been with a man. I was Mad at the time.
Mary Rogerson was present at the time. I had to kill her.

It had been one of those cases that haunt the public imagination, and in the streets and playgrounds the children chanted their own summary in rhyme:

Red stains on the carpet, red stains on the knife,
For Doctor Buck Ruxton had murdered his wife.
The maidservant saw it and threatened to tell,
So Doctor Buck Ruxton he killed her as well.

Love Lives of the Medici Family

The great Medici family, merchants and bankers of Florence, are remembered both for their political eminence and their lavish patronage of the arts. Their love lives, however, left a very great deal to be desired. Take Cosimo I, Grand Duke of Tuscany (1519–74). He cruelly poisoned his faithless wife Eleanor of Toledo after having her lover done to death. It is said that Cosimo later rejoiced in the brutal double murder, boasting openly that 'killing the bull first and the cow after made the sacrifice all the more pleasing.'

Cosimo himself enjoyed the favours of his own daughter, the beautiful and intelligent Isabella. The artist Vasari once witnessed their incest while painting a ceiling at the Palazzo Vecchio. There was a dark moment afterwards when Cosimo suddenly remembered that the painter might be at work, and climbed the scaffolding dagger in hand. But Vasari prudently pretended to be asleep and so escaped assassination.

Isabella was married to the Duke of Bracciano. However, she enjoyed an illicit liaison with Troilus Orsini, one of her husband's bodyguards. When her lover got her pregnant he fled to France, but was tracked down there by Bracciano's men and murdered. Isabella sought protection with her loving father Cosimo, who sheltered both her and her illegitimate child. Bracciano did not dare to take his revenge on his wife immediately. Not long after Cosimo's death, however, Bracciano lured Isabella to his estate at Cerreto. There, on 16 July 1576, he strangled her.

Gothic Horror
Lord Bernage of Sivray, Chief Groom to France's Charles VIII in the 15th century, witnessed a lamentable sight while serving as ambassador in Germany. A noble lady there could be seen in the evenings drinking from a human skull.

It was the skull of her lover. The wretched woman was forced to sip from it by her vengeful husband who had murdered the miscreant.

Cosimo de' Medici

The Worm That Turned

The French have a useful expression to describe a certain sort of husband in a love-triangle quarrel. The term is *mari complaisant* (complaisant husband) and it refers to a man who is perfectly aware of his wife's adultery but meekly acquiesces in it. He is a stock figure of fun in French fiction and folklore, and recurs time and again in real-life cases.

One such was René de Villequier, an eminent nobleman in the court of Henri III. For some 15 years he tolerated the infidelities of his wife Françoise de la Marck. He knew all about the life she was leading, occasionally remonstrated with her, but also harnessed her appetites to serve his own political career.

Attending the court at Poitiers on the morning of 1 September 1577, de Villequier went into his wife's bedroom and after joining her between the sheets, joking and laughing with her, he gave her four or five thrusts with a dagger. He called one of his men to finish her off. Then, having stabbed a maidservant for good measure, he had his wife's body placed in a litter which was paraded before the king and his nobles.

Having taken the corpse back to his house for burial, de Villequier returned and put in an appearance at court. There he triumphed in his avenged honour. He declared that he would gladly have killed her lovers too, but since they formed a small army there might be difficulties.

Henri III records the scandal in his *Journal*, and censures both the killer and his victim. But of course, no action was taken against de Villequier. They have always been funny like that, the French.

All in the Family

When West German building firm owner Hans Appel married Renate Poeschke, each brought to the household a child by a previous marriage. Then Renate bore Hans a daughter – and the family expanded further when in 1973, Renate's brother Juergen moved in.

Hans made a shattering discovery one night as he was putting the children to bed. One of the infants confided that mummy and uncle Juergen had spent an afternoon in bed together – with no clothes on.

Incest possesses a power to shock as perhaps no other sexual transgression. Hans was appalled, but when he confronted the guilty couple neither replied with a firm denial. Instead, brother and sister quit the household and moved into the Sachsenhausen home of 21-year-old Dieter Poeschke. He was Renate's other brother, a garage mechanic and a married man.

The construction boss was still in love with his wife despite what he now suspected. While giving her presents to try and win her back, he also took to carrying a revolver. But he remained on good terms with Dieter Poeschke. On 7 January 1974, Appel accepted a lift in his brother-in-law's Mercedes which was going from Wiesbaden to Frankfurt.

As the car travelled along the road, Hans Appel unburdened himself of his problems. It seemed incredible, he said, but he suspected that Renate was having an affair with Juergen. Did Dieter believe such a thing?

'Of course,' replied the driver, 'Juergen and I both sleep with Renate all the time.'

Double incest! Appel was to say that something inside him snapped at that point. Witnesses saw the car swerve onto a pavement. Dieter rolled out and as he staggered to his feet, Appel shot him twice with the pistol. Then the outraged husband got out of the Mercedes and disappeared down the street.

It did not take the police long to discover the killer's identity. But the bizarre circumstances of this particular crime of passion provided strong mitigating factors. Tried in July 1974, Appel was sentenced to 21 months imprisonment. In fact, he never served any time at all, for the sentence was set aside on appeal.

As for Renate, she would not return to her husband but went on living with her brother Juergen.

Chapter
Three

Miscellaneous
Mayhem

Not every crime of passion involves murder; many a lesser
misdemeanour is rooted in thwarted love. The peace may
be breached by a spring-heeled husband or calamitous
kidnap attempt. More serious cases too may retain
elements of grotesque comedy, as in the extraordinary
affair of the Missing Mormon. Even murder itself may
entertain – at a distance – through bizarre circumstances
or consequences. Such at least was the case of Oxford's
debt of dishonour, paid out over seven hundred years.
Everyone is a fool in love, and rampant passion does
not only appall. It may amuse, intrigue – or frankly
astonish – by exposing humanity's foibles.

The Missing Mormon

If a Mormon missionary were suspected of raping a beauty queen, the affair would provide ample material for sensational news treatment. But when, in 1977, a beauty queen was suspected of raping a Mormon missionary, the case had all the makings of a grand press block-buster. The newspapers went wild over the saga of Kirk Anderson and Joyce McKinney, devoting such an acreage of newsprint to it at one stage that the *Daily Mail* was constrained to advertise itself as 'The Paper *Without* Joyce McKinney'.

The story first broke in September 1977, with the disappearance and subsequent reappearance of American missionary Kirk Anderson. The *Sunday Times* noted on the 18th of that month:

> The Mormon missionary missing in Surrey turned up yesterday and said he had been kidnapped and held handcuffed and manacled for three days – it is believed on the orders of a wealthy, lovesick woman.
>
> Kirk Anderson, 21, was released unharmed near Victoria Station in London and telephoned Scotland Yard to say he was returning to his home at Milton Gardens, Epsom, by train. However, he boarded the wrong train and ended up at Sutton a few miles away, and had to call the police to pick him up.

That slip-up by the luckless missionary was a portent of stranger things to come. Anderson told the police of how he had long been persecuted by a 29-year-old former girlfriend named Joyce McKinney. They had had a brief affair in Salt Lake City, the Mormons' worldwide headquarters, and when he broke with her she had begun to harass him. The missionary alleged that windows at his home had been smashed, car tyres ripped up and a car he was driving in was rammed. He moved from Utah to California – the girl followed him. After continued harassment, the Mormon asked to be sent to Britain to avoid her. But she would not give up. Anderson kept on running: from East Grinstead, to Reading and finally to Epsom.

It was at Epsom, the Mormon claimed, that the kidnapping had occurred.

'This seems to have been a case of hell hath no fury like a woman scorned', said the detective who had headed the search for Anderson. At Orem, in Utah, Anderson's parents declared their relief on hearing that their son was safe. 'We don't know anything about this girl', said Mrs Anderson. 'I personally think he has been living very close to the Lord.'

Joyce McKinney was arrested some time later, with a male accomplice named Keith Joseph May, aged 24. They were charged with abducting

Anderson, and, on a second charge, accused of possessing an imitation .38 revolver with intent to commit an offence. It was made known that Joyce McKinney had entered Britain on a false passport. Yet the first press accounts gave the impression of a tearful ingénue. From the back of the prison van taking her to court, the girl protested her innocence, handing out messages written on pages of the Bible. One read: 'Please ask Christians to pray for me.'

It was at a preliminary hearing in November that the salacious details on the affair started to hit the headlines. The 'Sex-in-Chains' case swept all other issues from the front pages of the popular press.

Opening for the prosecution, Anderson's counsel described the couple's brief affair in Utah in 1975, and Joyce McKinney's subsequent persecutions. He alleged that on 14 September, the girl and her accomplice had forced Anderson into a car outside his church, using an imitation revolver and a bottle of chloroform. The car sped off to a cottage in Devon where it arrived some five hours later. Miss McKinney had then told her captive that she was not going to let him go until he agreed to marry her.

There was no doubt that sexual intercourse had taken place at the cottage. Nor was there any doubt that Anderson was tied to a bed while the act took place. The point at issue was that Anderson claimed to have been the victim of forced sex, while McKinney alleged that the shackles were merely instruments of bondage games.

In Anderson's version, Keith May had fastened him to the bed with chains and a leather strap. 'Joy told me if there was to be a ransom, the ransom would be that I would have to give her a baby.' Asked how female rape could have occurred, Anderson replied: 'She had oral sex'.

On the third night of his captivity, the missionary said, he was completely spread-eagled on the bed: 'When she came into the room there was a fire in the fireplace and she put some music on. She was wearing a négligée. She came to me as I lay on the bed. I said I would like to have my back rubbed. She proceeded to do that but I could tell she wanted to have intercourse again. I said I did not.' She left and returned with Keith May who used chains, ropes and padlocks to tie him down on his back to the four corners of the bed. She tore the pyjamas from his body and had her way with him.

Anderson firmly refuted the suggestion that the bondage equipment was for sex games. But the back rub? Wasn't that highly erotic, and bound to court temptation? Anderson was aggrieved: 'I do not look at a back rub like that. My mom gives me a pretty good back rub, but that does not mean that I want sex with her.'

During cross-questioning, Anderson alluded to a bizarre accessory of his own – an article of clothing unknown to the general public. This was the Mormons' sacred undergarment.

Above: McKinney outside Epsom Court; Right: Anderson leaving court

Not only had Miss McKinney torn off his pyjamas; she had also violated a special one-piece undergarment which acted as a kind of male chastity belt. Anderson had since burnt the article. 'They are so sacred to me that anytime they are desecrated in any way the proper method to dispose of them is to burn them.'

Joyce McKinney's statements presented a very different version of events. Anderson had made love willingly, she said. They had indulged in oral sex and bondage games to sort out his sexual difficulties; he was lying, now, because he feared excommunication from the Mormon church.

'Mr Anderson lay willingly while I tied him up,' she said. 'If he had not, this little 120 lb girl could not have tied up a 250 lb, 6 ft 2 in man.' She was, in fact, terrified of Anderson's strength: 'His legs are as big round as my waist.' The missionary had revelled in the proceedings, and lay on the bed 'grinning like a monkey' and moving his hips with her.

McKinney invoked her own religious faith in her defence, claiming that back in Utah she had prayed for 'a very special boy' to come into her life. Anderson had 'teased me and kissed me until I was out of my mind.' In a much-quoted phrase, she declared: 'I loved Kirk so much I would have skiied down Mount Everest in the nude with a carnation up my nose.'

What was the public to make of it all? On the one hand, McKinney's protestations that 'this little girl' could not have tied down and ravished the hulking missionary carried some weight. But then, if Anderson was willing, what was Keith May's role in the affair? Her accomplice remained a somewhat shadowy figure. May's own counsel claimed that the Devon escapade was seen by his client as 'a rescue operation from the oppressive and tyrannical organisation' (the Mormon Church).

In all events, May and McKinney were granted bail prior to the trial proper, on condition that McKinney stayed indoors from 21.00 to 09.00 every night. On 13 March 1978, the conditions were eased so that the two defendants could go to the cinema in the evenings. The prosecution objected on the grounds that they might skip bail and flee the country. Nonsense, a spokesman for Miss McKinney insisted: 'She wants to remain in this country to clear her name.'

On 16 April, however, the world learned that the *Sex-in-Chains Girl* was missing. The police searched high and low – but to no avail.

What had happened was that, posing as a deaf mute, Joyce McKinney had fled to Canada. Safely across the Atlantic, having lost none of her old flair, she came out of hiding dressed as a nun.

The whole furore erupted again. Newspapers battled for exclusive interviews, and a legal war was waged between *Penthouse* (which claimed her own story) and the *Daily Express* (which published photographs and stories before the magazine reached the bookstalls). May 22 became Joyce McKinney Day as far as the popular press was concerned. The *Daily Mirror* managed to obtain a photograph of her in the nude. Lacking a comparable illustration, *The Sun* improvised by mocking up a montage of its own. Joyce McKinney's head was shown superimposed on the body of a naked woman skiing down snowy slopes – a carnation, of course, was shown protruding from a nostril.

'The gospel according to Mormon sex-in-chains girl Joyce McKinney is: Give a man what he wants,' blared the paper, and quoted the fugitive as saying, 'I'm a very old-fashioned girl. I believe that a man's home is his castle and that a husband should be pampered. All I wanted to do with Kirk was to satisfy and pleasure him. But he had deep inhibitions due to his upbringing. I wanted to get rid of those guilt feelings by doing sexually outrageous things to him in bed. I thought I had succeeded, but in the end the Mormon Church won.'

In reality, Joyce McKinney emerged as an all-American product. She was still remembered in North Carolina as a 'fine, fine girl', who had been a regular attender at Bible camp. As for being a beauty queen, the most that could be said was that she had once been elected Miss North Carolina High School. Her own account of her early affair with the missionary was described in true teen-magazine style. She had been out driving with a friend in her new Stingray convertible when the Mormon put his head through the window. 'I found myself gazing into the deepest pair of baby-blue eyes. He put Paul Newman to shame. My heart did flip-flops. I turned to my girlfriend and said: "Hey, get out – I'm in love"'. And of the affair which followed, Miss McKinney said: 'It was bombs, firecrackers, the Fourth of July every time he kissed me'.

Even her subsequent pursuit of the missionary seems to have been undertaken with a kind of blue-eyed innocence. According to a friend, she had visited skin-flicks and live sex acts in order to pick up tips on arousal. Then she placed an advertisement in an underground paper asking for 'a muscle man, a pilot and a preacher to help in a romantic adventure.' The proposed team was never assembled, but she managed to finance the trip to England with $15,000 paid to her by an insurance company for injuries received in a car crash.

Joyce McKinney's crime, if crime it was, had an ancient pedigree. She loved, not wisely, but too well. And after the last great orgy of confessions and interviews, the story died practically overnight. As far as the legal position was concerned, the fugitive forfeited her bail money, but proposals to extradite her for trial were abandoned.

For seven years, the case was almost forgotten. Then, in June 1984, newspapers announced, 'SEX-IN-CHAINS JOYCE IS AT IT AGAIN.' Incredibly, Joyce McKinney had hit the headlines for a new alleged harassment of Kirk Anderson. She was arrested in a car outside the ex-missionary's office at Salt Lake City, charged with disturbing the peace and giving false information to the police.

Anderson had married since the alleged kidnapping episode, and now worked for an airline company in Utah. It was the first time he had seen her in seven years. Anderson claimed that he had noticed Joyce shadowing him over the weekend and had stalked him to his office. He told police that he was very concerned she might be planning to snatch him again. A police spokesman said, 'When we arrested her we found a notebook detailing his every move. There were also pictures of Kirk and his wife Linda.'

A man was with Miss McKinney when the police swooped, but he was not arrested. Her lawyer, Jim Barber, said, 'She only wanted to see him for old times sake. She is writing a screenplay about her experiences and wanted to find out how the story ended.'

Appalling Assault by an Amazon

Absurd and terrible scenes were witnessed at the wedding of M. Augustin. The 45-year-old Parisian presented himself in 1871 to be married at the local mairie to a lovely young girl of 18. And the ceremony had just been concluded when the door of the hall burst open and a lady of gigantic stature stormed into the room and elbowed her way through the guests. Trailing behind her was a thin young lady of about 15 years old.

M. Augustin was a very little man.

'Wretch! Scoundrel!' cried the Amazon, addressing the diminutive groom. 'This is how you leave me in the lurch – I who have sighed during fifteen years for the day when I might call myself your wife!'

The groom turned as white as a sheet. The giantess grabbed him by the collar and jerked him up under her arm. Addressing the mayor in a voice like thunder, she boomed: 'Do I arrive too late?'

'The marriage is concluded', replied the official. 'Please put M. Augustin down.'

'Not without giving his deserts to the villain who leaves me with this girl.'

'No, no, that girl is not mine', piped the groom. This was a mistake.

'Repeat what you have said,' fumed the giantess, 'this child who is as like you as one pea is another – is she yours or not?'

M. Augustin made no reply. His persecutor then seized him by the nose and twisted it violently. Wedding guests tried to come to the man's aid, but the enraged woman now flailed him around like a battleaxe, forcing them back. In the furore which followed the mayor could be heard calling for the police, but the giantess at last relented.

'You need not give yourself the trouble. I will let go the rascal of my own accord.' Turning to the bride she said hoarsely: 'Here, my beauty, is your little bit of a man. I have not broken him. We have no further business here. Follow me, Baptistine.'

So saying she flung her victim at the foot of two policemen who just then appeared at the door. Then, muttering further terrible imprecations, she swept out with her daughter.

M. Augustin had fainted. But such was the awe of the wedding guests that nobody dared touch him until the last echo of heavy footsteps had died away in the distance. At last, they raised him to his feet and the assembly broke up in an atmosphere of silent gloom.

Debt Settled – 770 Years Later!

Student Slays His Mistress; a routine crime of passion, you might think. But sometimes the fascination of a case lies more in its aftermath than in the event itself. When one such murder occurred in mediaeval Oxford it helped to establish the world-famous university. And it led to a debt of dishonour paid, year in and year out, for more than seven centuries.

It all began in 1209, when a student at the newly founded university murdered his mistress, a woman of the town. The miscreant made a quick getaway. And the mayor and people responded in a rage by stringing up a couple of students in his place.

In compensation for the lynching, the papal legate ordered the town of Oxford to do penance, to feast the poorer students annually, and to excuse all scholars half of their rent annually for a space of ten years. Additionally, a yearly fine of 52 shillings was imposed on the townsfolk.

Few crimes of passion can have had more long-lived consequences. Payment began in 1214, the cash being deposited in a chest at St Mary's church. It amounted to a considerable sum which for a long time was about the only income the University possessed. The once-despised, starveling scholars became privileged people. They took to swaggering about the streets, and terrible Town and Gown riots resulted.

The fine itself continued to be paid annually for 770 years. The industrial revolution transformed the nation, the British Empire came and went, world wars were fought, men walked on the moon – and still the ancient blood money was paid *propter suspendium clericorum* (for the hanging of the clerks).

The Treasury had by now taken on the debt, calculated at £3.08 per annum. It was payable to the University Chest, and it was the duty of the Vice Chancellor to administer the sum for the relief of poor students. And this curious thread in the tapestry of history was not snapped until June 1984.

In that month, as part of an efficiency drive at the Treasury, a final payment was agreed on. The government presented the University with its last cheque – £33.08 as a once-for-all settlement of the account.

Mr William Hyde, secretary of the Chest, regretted the decision: 'We have not really any choice in the matter. They decided to buy it out. It's a pity from the nostalgic point of view to see the end of a 700-year payment of this nature.' But he agreed that no strong case could be made for perpetuating the debt of dishonour. Besides, he conceded, 'three pounds does not relieve a lot of poverty.'

Passionate Phantoms

A 17th century tombstone at Chagford church in Devon commemorates the death of Mary Whiddon. The unhappy girl was shot dead by a jealous lover, at the altar on her wedding day. A dramatic end to a love-triangle quarrel – but is it entirely ended? To this day, it is said, the ghost of the young bride haunts her home at Chagford. The building today is a guest house, and more than one visitor has been startled to see the wraith of a young woman in black smiling sadly from the doorway of what used to be Mary's room.

You don't have to believe in ghosts to appreciate how deeply memories of love tragedy have rooted themselves in the folklore of the nation. After the death of

Mrs Rattenbury (see page 163), her shrouded spectre was reported on several occasions to haunt the lonely scene of her end by the River Avon. The apparition was so often witnessed that in October 1935, the famous ghost-hunter Elliott O'Donnell spent a night's vigil in the misty watermeadow. An eerie experience – the investigator saw no phantom, but he did experience an overwhelming urge to drown himself in the river.

Longleat, the nation's most famous stately home, is reputedly haunted by a spectral Green Lady who frequents a certain corridor. She has been identified as Lady Louisa Cartaret, 18th century wife of the 2nd Viscount Weymouth. He killed her young lover in a furious fight fought out in the haunted corridor. Afterwards, so the story has always told, he buried the body in the cellar. Pure fairytale? Yet early in the 20th century, the cellar was excavated to lay pipes for central heating – and the skeleton of a man in 18th century riding boots was discovered under the flagstones.

The mostly widely reported spectral victim of love tragedy, though, is the ghost of Anne Boleyn. The ill-fated queen has been sighted at a number of old manors around the country, each claiming to be her birthplace. And nowhere does the apparition make a more spectacular appearance than at Blickling Hall in Norfolk. Every year on the anniversary of the queen's execution (19 May 1536) a spectral coach is said to convey Anne's ghost up to the door of the hall. The cortege arrives at midnight: the coachman is headless; the four horses are headless; Anne too is headless, of course, bearing the severed item upon her lap.

Chapter
Four

Carefully laid plans

You might think that every crime of passion is committed on the impulse of the moment. Yet even in the classic cases, some premeditation may be involved in, for example, the purchase of a knife or gun. How long, after all, is a moment to an obsessed or injured lover: a split-second, an hour, a day? Sometimes, it seems, molten passion may be contained for longer still while the brain – soaring in some stratosphere of icy calm – maps out a scheme of vengeance.

The crimes in this section were all ones in which evidence of careful planning was brought before the courts. Sometimes that evidence was questionable, as in the tragedy of Edith Thompson. More often it was substantial enough. An Italian vet, a New Zealand justice minister and a French duke of noblest line are among the patient planners whose schemes ultimately went awry.

The Black Perambulator

The woman was found in a Hampstead street, lying on a heap of builders' rubbish. Moonlight played softly on her black jacket with its trimming of imitation Astrakhan. Her skull was crushed, and head itself had almost been severed from the body – it remained attached only by a sliver of skin and muscle.

The date was 24 October 1890, and rumours soon started to circulate. It was whispered that the murder was the work of Jack the Ripper, the phantasmal figure who had stalked the East End only two years earlier. Had the Ripper now returned to claim victims in North London?

A mile or so away was an abandoned perambulator whose cushions were soaked with blood. And the following day, detectives made another grim discovery. The corpse of an 18-month-old baby was recovered from waste ground in Finchley. It was not very long before the three gruesome finds were connected.

The murdered woman was found to have the initials P.H. embroidered on her underclothes. The fact was reported in a morning newspaper which caught the attention of a certain Clara Hogg, who lived in Kentish Town. She knew that her sister-in-law, Mrs Phoebe Hogg, had gone out on the afternoon of 24 October with her baby. She had not come back that night. The initials fitted the missing woman, and Clara went with a friend to the mortuary where the body had been taken. There, choking back her nausea, Clara recognised her sister-in-law as the grisly figure on the slab.

What puzzled the police was the behaviour of Clara's friend, a tall redheaded woman named Mary Pearcey. She insisted that the corpse was not Phoebe Hogg's; she became hysterical and tried to drag Clara away. It was, in fact, to visit Mary Pearcey that Phoebe Hogg had set out on the fateful afternoon. Yet the russet-haired Mary first denied the fact; then admitted that the visit had taken place.

Clearly, Mary Pearcey's role in the affair needed some investigation. And it did not take much probing for detectives to discover a familiar geometry in the mystery – the geometry of a love triangle.

Frank Hogg, husband of the murdered Phoebe, turned out to be a man with an eye for the ladies. A bearded and jovial furniture remover, he had lived with his wife at Prince of Wales Road, Kentish Town. But Frank also possessed the latchkey to Mary's home at Priory Road nearby. He was a regular visitor there, and had been since before his marriage.

Probing deeper, the police discovered that the marriage itself was a forced affair. While he was still a bachelor in 1888, Frank had been seeing both women. His true affection was for the strong-willed and vivacious Mary Pearcey. It was, however, the meeker Phoebe Styles who became pregnant by him. Although leading a double love-life, Frank was a regular church-goer who knew which course he ought to pursue. He wrestled for some time with his conscience, at one point proposing to abandon the whole mess by making a new life abroad. It was Mary Pearcey who told him not to emigrate, but to marry the pregnant Phoebe. The redhead wrote him passionate letters which expressed little jealousy of her rival: 'Oh, Frank! I should not like to think I was the cause of all your troubles, and yet you make me think so. What can I do? I love you with all my heart, and I will love her because she will belong to you.'

Again: 'Do not think of going away, for my heart will break if you do; don't go dear. I won't ask too much, only to see you for five minutes when you can get away; but if you go quite away, how do you think I can live? I would see you get married 50 times over – yes, I could bear that far better than parting with you for ever . . . you must not go away. My heart throbs with pain only to think about it.'

Mixed in with these protestations of love were phrases culled from the romantic novelettes which Mary read avidly. One has an especially ironic ring in retrospect: 'In this false world we do not always know who are our friends and who our enemies, and all need friends . . .'

In the end, Frank did marry Phoebe Styles, settling down with her, his mother and sister Clara at Prince of Wales Road. Phoebe seems to have known all about her husband's liaison with Mary, but raised no strong objections to it. Curiously, the two women were friends, and when Phoebe's second child miscarried, Mary even nursed her rival through the pain and trauma. As for the first baby, Mary doted on it, almost as if she shared in the motherhood of the infant in every way.

To this day, what triggered the bloody climax remains a mystery. The police did determine, though, that on the day before the fateful visit, Mary sent Phoebe a note: 'Dearest: come round this afternoon and bring our little darling, don't fail.' On that occasion, the blinds at Mary's house were seen to be drawn down as if in preparation. As it happened, Phoebe Hogg was unable to go round that day, but after receiving a second note she went to the house the following day.

Mary did admit to police that Phoebe arrived with the baby in the pram, but claimed it was only to borrow some money. Asked why she had first denied the visit, she replied improbably: 'I did not tell you before because Phoebe asked me not to let anybody know that she had been here.' Later, to a police matron, she was to hint that there had been an argument: 'As we were having tea Mrs Hogg made some remark which I did not like – one word brought up another. Perhaps I had better not say any more.'

THE WORLD'S GREATEST CRIMES OF PASSION

The neighbours had heard screaming in Mary Pearcey's house at 16.00 – screaming, and the smashing of crockery.

The police produced a search warrant and examined the premises. They found that they had been recently cleaned, but not very thoroughly. Spatters of blood could be seen on the walls and ceiling; the poker had blood and hairs on it. In a dresser drawer was a carving knife, also stained with blood. A skirt, an apron, curtains, a rug – all bore tell-tale stains.

Mary Pearcey sat at a piano during the search, and tinkled out nursery rhymes. When asked why so many bloodstains were to be found about the place she continued to play at the keyboard, eerily chanting, 'Killing mice, killing mice, killing mice!'

Later, the police discovered that Mary was wearing two wedding rings; no ring had been found on the body of Phoebe Hogg.

Arrested and charged with murder, 24-year-old Mary Pearcey was tried at the Old Bailey in December 1890. Throughout the proceedings, the accused woman protested her innocence, but the circumstantial evidence against her was overwhelming. Some two hours after the cries were heard at her home, a neighbour had seen Mary Pearcey pushing the perambulator, draped with a black shawl, along Priory Road. Night had now fallen, and she was hunched over the vehicle as if hoping not to be recognised. The pram itself appeared heavily laden, with something strangely bulky crammed up towards the hood . . .

The extraordinary journey which followed covered a circuit of some six miles. The murdered woman was found at Crossfield Road, Hampstead, and the baby was abandoned off Finchley Road. There was no evidence of violence done to the infant, but its clothing was stained with blood. The impression was that it may have been suffocated by the weight of the corpse above it. As for the perambulator, it was found abandoned in Hamilton Terrace, St John's Wood, its grim freight shed at last.

Frank Hogg admitted to the police that he had gone round to Priory Road late that night, and let himself in with his latchkey. When he found the place empty, he pencilled a brief note: 'Twenty past ten. Cannot stay.' Had he lingered, he might have encountered Mary Pearcey returning from her macabre excursion.

The jury took only an hour to consider its verdict and found Mary Eleanor Pearcey guilty of murder. Asked if she had anything to say why sentence of death should not be passed, she swiftly answered: 'Only that I am innocent of the charge.'

Now wretched and reviled, Frank Hogg refused to see his mistress in the condemned cell, a rebuff which Mary lamented: 'He might have made death easier to bear.' On 23 December 1890 she was led to the scaffold and she faced her end with great calm and composure. To the prison chaplain accompanying her, she observed enigmatically: 'The sentence is just; the evidence was false.'

A puzzling remark. And it is just one of the untidy strands left in the Pearcey case. Some have doubted whether Mary could have accomplished the crime alone: Phoebe had been clubbed senseless and had her head severed by a knife drawn across the throat several times. It was done with such force that it cut clean through the vertebrae. Then there was the business of cramming the corpse into the pram. This was a formidable task even granted the point made by F. Tennyson Jesse in her *Murder and Its Motives*: 'the matter was made easier by the fact that there was nothing to prevent the head being doubled right back.'

What provoked the maniacal assault? Was it premeditated, or sparked by that 'remark which I did not like'? And if the evidence was false, who had falsified it?

London in the 1890s was the city of yellow fog and gaslit streets known to readers of Sherlock Holmes stories. And for afficionados of great unsolved murder mysteries there is one tantalizing postscript piece which in no way fits the jigsaw.

It emerged at the trial that Mary Pearcey's true name was Mary Eleanor Wheeler. She had taken her surname from that of a carpenter, John Charles Pearcey, with whom she had once cohabited. He stated at the trial that they were never formally married, and that he had left Mary because of her roving eye. But some mysterious figure seems to have occupied a special place in her affections. For on the day of her execution, Mary instructed her solicitor to place the following advertisement in the Madrid newspapers: 'M.E.C.P. Last wish of M.E.W. Have not betrayed.'

There is little doubt that Mary Pearcey lured Phoebe Hogg to Priory Road and there killed the unfortunate woman. The motive seems clearly to have been rooted in jealous love. Who then was M.E.C.P.? And what was the secret they shared? The puzzle has prompted one fantastic solution: that Mary was a member of a nefarious secret society, and liquidated Phoebe when she found out about it. More prosaically, it has been suggested that Mary was secretly married as a teenager to a man whose name she did not want sullied at the trial. Finally, it is possible that the novelette-reading Mary simply invented a little enigma to lend romance to her appalling crime.

We simply do not know. But reading and re-reading the last cryptic message you cannot help believing that a fascinating dimension to the case of Mary Pearcey may have dropped into the void when the hangman's fatal trap was sprung.

A Crime That Rocked a Kingdom

It was an odd, odd business. The scandal that rocked France in 1847 helped to bring down a dynasty. It involved one of the noblest families in the nation, and no *crime passionnel* in French history has provoked more discussion. There is no question about the identity of the murderer in the Praslin affair, nor of the horrific savagery of the crime. Thick dossiers of letters and statements still survive in the Paris National Archives, along with trunkloads of material evidence: a silken bell pull, bloodstained clothing, bronze candlesticks and a hunting knife among other items. But despite all that has survived and all that has been written, mystery lingers about the case, elusive as the aroma of expensive tobacco and the musk of Old French roses. Underneath, it was an odd, odd business.

The young Théobald de Praslin married Fanny Sébastiani on 19 October 1824. He was only nineteen, she was two years younger, and they were very much in love at the time. The families on both sides being of immense wealth, the wedding was a glittering occasion. The young marquis was heir to the great Praslin dukedom, and his bride was an honorary goddaughter of Napoleon. Big interests blessed the marriage, which began rich in promise as an idyl of domestic happiness.

She bore him children – nine of them in less than fifteen years – perhaps too many in the light of what was to come. For under the strain of successive pregnancies and births, the Marquise lost her radiant looks. Her dark, romantic features – inherited from Corsican blood – thickened and became swart. She grew corpulent. And her temperament, once agreeably capricious, soured into a volatile and domineering nature.

Her husband, in contrast, was a passive, introverted man little given to displays of emotion. The more she nagged, ranted and threw tantrums the more he retreated into a shell of cold reserve. Fanny continued to love Théobald in her tempestuous fashion; but on his part, love turned slowly into detestation.

Before 1839, when their last child was born, the decline in their relationship had begun. Already he had taken to shunning her bedroom, and she was writing him letters of complaint. They were eloquent letters which sprang directly from the heart, but the themes were monotonously reiterated: she regretted her fits of temper, tried to patch up the latest quarrel, craved his pity for her uncontrollable emotions. 'I am no longer the mistress of my feeling', she wrote at one point. 'Something over which I have no control takes possession of me.'

The Marquis merely became more disdainful. And in 1840, things took a terrible turn for the worse when he required her to sign an extraordinary document. By the terms of this private agreement, Madame de Praslin was to give up her natural rights as a mother. The family's governess was to have sole charge of all that concerned the children: clothes, schooling, recreation and so on. Madame de Praslin was not even permitted to see them unless in the company of the governess.

It was, by any standards, an appalling document for a mother to sign, and historians have long puzzled over its implications. Madame de Praslin wrote privately about it, claiming that she had sacrificed all to try and regain her husband's affection. But there are hints that some specific incident or discovery lay behind her renunciation. Was it some violent outburst which had frightened the children and led her husband to think them unsafe in her presence? Or was it something darker than that?

A charge of somehow 'corrupting' the children seems to have been laid against Madame de Praslin. It is known that her own governess at one time had been a certain Madamoiselle Mendelssohn, suspected of lesbian relations with her pupils. Did the Marquis suspect his wife of the same proclivities? Had she interfered with her own children?

It is just one of the affair's lingering mysteries. The contract, the shunned bedroom – all this was in private. In public, the couple continued to appear amid the plush and chandeliers of the Court, to receive guests and dispense their hospitality. In June 1841, Théobald's father died and he became the fifth Duc de Choiseul-Praslin, inheriting not only some nine million francs but the magnificent château of Vaux-le-Vicomte.

This superb building survives as one of the great splendours of French Baroque style. With its domes and towers, fountains and tree-lined avenues, it was to provide the grandest backdrop imaginable for the drama which was to unfold.

To Vaux, with the new Duke and Duchess, came a new governess only recently hired. The orphaned and illegitimate daughter of a Bonapartist soldier, she had dragged herself out of a miserable childhood to serve with a noble English family. Fair-haired, green-eyed and socially accomplished, she came to the Praslins with the best possible credentials. In due course, the whole of France was to become fascinated by the Mademoiselle: her name was Henriette Deluzy.

Partisans of the Duchess were to paint her as a scheming adventuress who brought shame to a noble household. Others saw her as a decent girl placed in an intolerable position. History's verdict must draw a little from each portrait. Henriette Deluzy did not create the unhappy marriage – it was in a disastrous state when she arrived. Nor (this seems quite clear) did she and the Duke ever become lovers in the carnal sense. But the pretty young governess was both intelligent and ambitious. Coming from her own insecure background, the splendours of Vaux, the Praslin millions, all the ranks and privileges which went with them – these lures combined with the manifest unhappiness of the Duke must surely have excited her thoughts. After all, even decent girls may dream a little . . .

Praslin told her at the outset about the contract he had made with his wife. Though it struck her as strange, it also gave her unique powers in the household. Mademoiselle Deluzy accepted the position and was soon supervising all that concerned the children. Two of the daughters, Berthe and Louise, came quickly to adore her. The young instructress was bright, vivacious and thoroughly sane – in marked contrast to their unbalanced, faintly terrifying mother.

It was not long before the Duke, too, came to seek refuge from the chill of his marriage in the governess's warm little circle. He loved his children and he loved to see them happy. Temperamentally indolent as well as reticent, the Duke spent more and more time in their company.

The Duchess, of course, was reduced to paroxysms of rage. Mademoiselle Deluzy quickly became 'that woman', and night after night in her lonely bedchamber the Duchess wrote long impassioned letters to her husband. The governess, she fumed, was 'bold, familiar, dominating, thoughtless, inquisitive, gossipy, insolent and greedy.' She had split the family, and set daughters against their mother. One accusation repeatedly made is of especial significance in the light of what was to come. The Duchess claimed that the scheming governess was deliberately *making it appear* as if she was her husband's mistress. The Duchess, however, never at any stage seems to have suspected that her rival was actually sharing his bed.

Everybody else, though, came to believe that she was. Within a year or so of Mlle Deluzy's arrival the rumours were beginning to spread. In a Paris society that drank gossip like fine wine, the scandal began to ferment. In the summer of 1844 the Duchess publicly threatened suicide, creating such an embarrassing scene that the Duke decided that a break was called for. He took three of his daughters, with their governess, off on a long Mediterranean holiday. The Duchess remained at Vaux. And for the first time in print, there appeared in a Paris gossip column, a snippet concerning the Praslin ménage. The Duke, it was said, had gone off for a vacation with his mistress.

This delicious little item did not go unnoticed. The story circulated not only around the Paris boulevards, but reached the courts of Europe as well. Mademoiselle Deluzy would have to leave the household now, all the well-informed tattlers said. But she did not. To do so would only give credence to the rumours, and the Duke determined to remain aloof from such malicious gossip.

Shamed beyond endurance, the humiliated Duchess took to eating all her

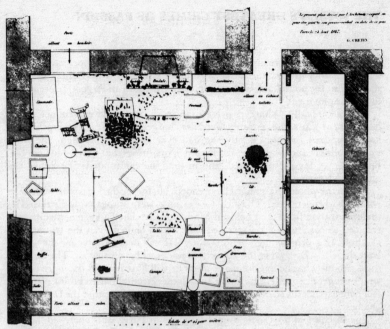

The bedroom of the Duchesse de Praslin

meals in the solitude of her bedchamber. She refused any contact with the governess and penned ever more eloquently hysterical letters to her husband.

The whole miserable business dragged on. In 1846, an unaccountable reconciliation appeared to occur, when the Duchess suddenly started making herself agreeable to the governess. It can only be explained as a change of tactics, though, for Madame de Praslin still fulminated in her letters to her husband about the 'little pair of green eyes behind your shoulder.' In reality, the mortified mother was maturing a plan for revenge.

She struck in June 1847. In that month, the Duke was suddenly but formally informed by his father-in-law that if the governess did not leave the household for good, his wife would sue for divorce and claim sole custody of the children.

The threat had terrible implications. The Duke himself clearly believed (for whatever reason) that his children were unsafe with their mother. Not only would he lose them to her, but the furore of the divorce would seriously affect his daughters' marriage prospects. The scandal would be immense, and what right-minded noble family would take on girls from this adulterous ménage? He could not doubt that Madame de Praslin would win her case – the scandal-mongering press had seen to that.

THE WORLD'S GREATEST CRIMES OF PASSION

Now the governess really did have to go. After a fierce but hopeless argument with his father-in-law, the Duke regretfully informed Mlle Deluzy that she should quit the household, with a generous life pension and a good reference for future employment.

She took it badly. Whatever private fancies she may have entertained about her future at Vaux, she certainly loved her charges; for six years the Praslin girls had comprised the only family she had ever known. That night she wept uncontrollably and swallowed laudanum in quantities that nearly took her life. But the next day she recovered, and in time she capitulated. She signed the annuity agreement.

And so the whole affair might have ended, but for the dark passions which the episode had engendered. The girls, for example, were unspeakably distressed by their separation from their beloved Mademoiselle. The Duke, meanwhile, was reduced to cold fury, a refrigerated rage which chilled even the triumphant Duchess. In a private memoir she wrote: 'He will never forgive me for what I have done . . . Every day the abyss between us will grow deeper. The more he thinks about what he has done, the more he will hate me and the more he will wreak vengeance on me. The future appalls me. I tremble when I think of it . . .'

There was not much of a future left, as it transpired, for either the Duke or the Duchess.

The discharged governess sought lodgings in Paris. But wherever she was accepted she would immediately find herself thrown back out onto the street. A certain Abbé Gallard was going the rounds, warning the owners off. Mlle Deluzy, said the cleric, was an immoral woman soon to be named in a divorce court. Also, he implied that she was pregnant. The Abbé Gallard was the Duchess's confessor.

Eventually, the embattled governess found a small room at the Pensionnat Lemaire, a school for young women in one of the seedier quarters of Paris. She was desperately unhappy and wrote pitiful letters to the Praslin girls imploring them not to forget her. They answered with equal *tendresse*: they had had terrible scenes with their mother, they wrote. Also: 'You are our real mother.'

On 26 July, Mlle Deluzy briefly met two of the Praslin children with their father in Paris. His face at that time seemed to have crumpled. And during the brief meeting he told the ex-governess something about the Duchess that quite appalled her.

We do not know what that something was.

It is another of the lingering mysteries. Among all the documents preserved in the National Archives, references to the dark secret seem to have been excised. From allusions that have survived it is known to have involved '*horrors*', 'secret carryings-on' and the Duchess's 'corruption of her sons'. Horace, the ten-year-old boy, had 'confessed infamies' to his father.

Some have interpreted these elusive references in the most literal way, suggesting that the Duchess had seduced at least one of her young sons. A more probable solution is proposed by Stanley Loomis in his authoritative study of the case, *A Crime of Passion* (1967). We know that after the governess had gone, the Duchess continued to threaten the divorce unless Mlle Deluzy actually left the country. That was what lay behind the persecutions of the Abbé Gallard. And it is possible that the Duchess had persuaded one or more of the boys to speak out against his father and the governess. He might even lie, pretending, for example, to have witnessed the couple in bed. Pure speculation, of course. What we do know is that the cold, reserved and rather weak-spirited Duke now plotted the murder of his wife.

All the pent rage inside him found expression in his plan of revenge. At the great Paris residence, the Hôtel Sébastiani, he began in the most comically inept way by removing the screws from his wife's bedposts. His idea was that the vast and weighty canopy above would collapse to crush or suffocate her. There is no doubt that he entertained this bizarre project, culled from the romantic fiction of the day. After the affair had reached its bloody climax, it was found that ceiling wax had been stuffed as camouflage into the holes where the screws had been.

Nor was this the Duke's sole preparation. At the Hôtel Sébastiani, he also used his trusty screwdriver to remove the bolt by which his wife could lock her door from his own connecting suite. If the canopy failed to kill the Duchess, he would then be guaranteed of access to finish the job. His plans made, the Duke gave orders that absolutely nobody should enter the Hôtel apartments until the next visit of his family to Paris.

That visit came on 17 August. While Madame de Praslin went straight to the Hôtel Sébastiani, the Duke and four of his children repaired first to the Pensionnat Lemaire for a tearful reunion with the discharged governess. During the brief call, the Duke promised that he would try and get letters of reference from the Duchess for Mademoiselle Deluzy.

Once back at the Hôtel, father and children retired to their various quarters. The lights were out by 23.30; all looked set for a peaceful night. It was at about 04.30 that a succession of blood-curdling, barely human shrieks ripped the dawn air over Paris.

The Duke, having perhaps waited hours for the canopy to collapse, had resorted to a furtive assault. He crept stealthily into his wife's bedroom, carrying with him a pistol and hunting knife. Bruises found on the corpse the following morning indicate that he clamped one hand firmly over her mouth as with the other he tried to cut her throat. But he only half-succeeded. With blood spurting from a gashed artery, Madame de Praslin woke and grabbed the double-edged blade, cutting her hand in the process. A big, strong woman, she managed to

A contemporary print depicting the death of the Duchess

break free, to scream and to tug at the bell rope. A horrific fight and chase ensued, the Duchess staggering like a wounded animal around the room, steadying herself against the walls with her bleeding hand, frantic to escape her maniacal husband. Chairs and tables were knocked over; the bell rope was torn from its mounting. Later that morning, the copious bloodprints all around enabled the police to map the whole struggle with fine precision. It was on the sofa before the fireplace that the fifth Duke of Choiseul-Praslin finally cornered his wife. There, using a weighty brass candlestick taken from the mantlepiece, he clubbed her to the ground.

From the moment that the first terrible yelp had filled the Hôtel, servants had been trying to break into the suite. But all the doors were locked. Eventually, it was the Duke himself who admitted the staff. 'What has happened?' he asked them, feigning ignorance. The Duchess died moments later, and though the Duke tried to brazen it out by claiming that an intruder must have been responsible, his guilt was quickly established. When the head of the Sûreté Nationale first examined the appalling scene he remarked: 'This is not the work of a professional. It is the work of a gentleman.'

The Duke had had time to try and destroy the evidence, but in no satisfactory way. Smoke was seen pouring from the fireplace in his own bedroom, where he had burned bits of bloodstained clothing as well as a quantity of papers. The *robe de chambre* he was wearing was found to be damp with water applied to the red bloodmarks on the material. His hands were scratched and bitten, and the hunting knife was found concealed in his apartment.

Paris was in uproar. A crowd gathered immediately around the Hôtel, and called for the death of the murderer. For the indignant citizenry, the crime came to embody all the moral corruption with which the régime was tainted. The constitutional monarchy of Louis-Philippe was already reeling from a financial scandal in which two government ministers had been implicated. The next year the king was to be overthrown by revolution; and historians have identified the Praslin murder as being a key event which helped to trigger the insurrection.

In the public mind the issue was clear: the Duke had murdered his wife for love of an English-trained governess. And the fear was that because of his rank, the murderer would escape punishment. In reality, there was no likelihood that this would happen. The Duke was brought to trial before a Court of Peers who fully recognised the need to appease the public. In fact, the peers' greatest worry was that the Duke might commit suicide before sentence could be passed. 'What a mess!' the king was heard to exclaim as he signed the order summoning the court to convene. For the government, Count Molé wrote to a colleague: 'Impress upon the Chancellor Pasquier (head of the court) that it will be a public misfortune if this monster escapes by a voluntary death the fate which the law has reserved for him.'

In the event, however, the Duke did deprive the court of the satisfaction of dispensing its justice. While under close guard, he managed to swallow a dose of arsenic. It took him six days to die of the poison – six days of atrocious agony. He remained tight-lipped to the end, answering only evasively the questions put to him, and refusing to confess his guilt.

All the weight of public interest now fell on Mademoiselle Deluzy. She was kept in confinement for three months after the murder and subjected to the most exhaustive questioning. Had she been the Duke's mistress? Had she encouraged the crime? Throughout her ordeal, the ex-governess remained adamant in her denials. In the end she was released a free woman, but with an official proclamation hanging over her. The document acknowledged that there was no evidence to connect her with the crime. It did, however, charge her with having had a 'culpable liaison' with the Duke.

A now notorious woman, Mademoiselle Deluzy left France in 1849 to make a new life in America. Wearied by her trials but unbroken in spirit, she there married a young Presbyterian minister named Henry Field. The couple became leading lights in New York's church community, and though her past was known it was not held against her. Mrs Field died in 1875 at the age of 63. The obituaries barely mentioned the Praslin affair, but fêted her for her generous hospitality, her good works and her shining intellect. Before she died she had even written about France for her husband's religious periodical, *The Evangelist*. In her articles Mrs Field expressed her conviction that, whatever political upheavals might rock the country of her birth, one quality would guarantee the survival and well-being of France.

That quality was the strength which the nation derived from its happy family life.

The Chalkpit Conspiracy

At dusk on 30 November 1946, a man walking the North Downs near Woldingham in Surrey saw what looked like a heap of old clothes lying in a secluded chalkpit. Curiosity prompted him to look closer; and he found that the clothes were inhabited. Lying rigid in the trench was the body of a young man, trussed by a rope around his neck. A dirty piece of green cloth was entangled in the noose; the dead man's face was purple. When the experts first examined the body, it looked very much like a case of suicide. Yet there was no tree from which he might have suspended himself. And, though his clothes were smeared with chalk and mud, his shoes were spotlessly clean. Maybe the body had been carried there for disposal.

In the victim's pocket was an old wartime identity card which declared him to be John McMain Mudie, 35. Recently demobbed, he was found to have been working as a barman at the Reigate Hill Hotel some 12 miles from the chalkpit. A handsome young man, well liked by all who knew him, Mudie was nobody's idea of a killer or a killer's victim. He was too plain decent to be mixed up in murder.

Painstaking detective work led the police to uncover a conspiracy hatched in London. Three men in particular were implicated. One was Lawrence John Smith, a joiner; the second, John William Buckingham, who ran a car hire business. And the third was a very much more august figure: he was Thomas John Ley, 66, colossally fat, and a former Minister of Justice in New Zealand. He had been a noted spokesman there for Prohibition, and was known as 'Lemonade Ley' in consequence.

Evidence against them included statements from two gardeners who had seen a man loitering suspiciously at the chalkpit on the day before Mudie disappeared. The man had driven away in a car whose registration plate bore the number 101. Smith had, it transpired, hired a Ford Eight, FGP 101, for three days over the murder period.

Then there was the rag found entangled in the noose. It had been torn from a French polisher's cloth found at 5 Beaufort Gardens, Kensington, where Thomas Ley lived. A pickaxe, moreover, was found at the chalkpit where it seemed to have been used in partially filling in the trench. This too was traced back to 5 Beaufort Gardens; it had served there for mixing concrete.

Significant evidence, all of it – but it needed something stronger to support it. That came on 14 December, when Buckingham turned King's Evidence.

The story that unfolded was one in which hot-blooded jealousy and cold calculation had conspired to produce a quite senseless killing. The ex-justice minister had, it appeared, long been involved in an affair with a widow from Perth named Mrs Maggie Brook. They had come to London in 1930 and pursued their liaison quite openly. At one time it had been a sexual relationship, but Ley had been impotent for a decade. His love had endured beyond his capacity, however. The couple saw each other as regularly as ever.

Mrs Brook, 66, emerged at the trial as a kindly and sweet-natured lady – no storybook scarlet woman. Ley, in contrast, was a blusterer and a bully consumed by quite irrational jealousy. He had accused his partner of having affairs with three separate young men at the Wimbledon house where she lodged. And one of these was the blameless Jack Mudie.

CAREFULLY LAID PLANS

Left: 5 Beaufort Gardens

**Below: Mrs Maggie Brook covers
her face to avoid the camera**

Mudie had not exchanged more than a dozen words with Mrs Brook; their contact extended to no more than chance greetings on the stairs or in the lobby. Perhaps the ex-justice minister had observed some such exchange. In all events, his suspicions were aroused.

Jealousy worked on Thomas Ley, spreading like an infection until it inflamed his whole being. By late November in 1946, Ley was toxic with it.

He contacted Smith, the joiner, who had helped convert his Beaufort Gardens house into flats. Buckingham was introduced to him as a man who could 'keep his mouth shut'. Ley told the pair that he wanted to kidnap a blackmailer who was persecuting a lady of his acquaintance. The man should be brought back to his house, tied up and forced to sign a confession. Smith and Buckingham did not ask too many questions. Ley offered them money – 'more than a year's salary' for each of them.

The plot involved finding a way of getting Mudie peacefully into the house. Buckingham came up with the idea of using a woman. She should turn up at Mudie's bar with a chauffeur and limousine. Complimenting the proposed victim on his bar-tending skills, she would invite him back to her house to help out with a cocktail party of her own. One Lilian Bruce was hired for the role, with Buckingham's son to play chauffeur. Smith and Buckingham senior would follow in a second car, overtaking just before Beaufort Gardens, so that they could prepare a reception committee. Ley himself would be waiting there too – waiting for the delivery of his victim.

All went as planned on the evening of 28 November. Smith and Buckingham got into the house first through the front door. Mudie was ushered in by the back entrance. Mrs Bruce and her chauffeur then immediately disappeared, leaving the barman to his fate.

Nearly 40 years have passed since the Chalkpit Conspiracy was exposed. Yet even today, it is not known precisely what transpired at Beaufort Gardens. Buckingham claimed that once Mudie was tied up, his own role in the affair was over. Ley gave him £200 in one pound notes, and he left straight away with the payment. Smith, though, stayed some ten minutes longer . . . and it was Smith who, with Thomas Ley, was charged with murder at the Old Bailey.

Both denied the murder charge. Smith's statement roughly agreed with Buckingham's; he said that he too had left with Mudie trussed but fully conscious. But he gave no satisfactory reason for lingering that extra ten minutes. Moreover, there were details which suggested that he knew very well that Mudie would not leave the house alive.

They had used the French polisher's rag to gag him. A rug had been thrown over the victim's head while he was being tied up. Mudie had cried out: 'you're stifling me.' And either Smith or Buckingham had retorted: 'you are breathing your last.'

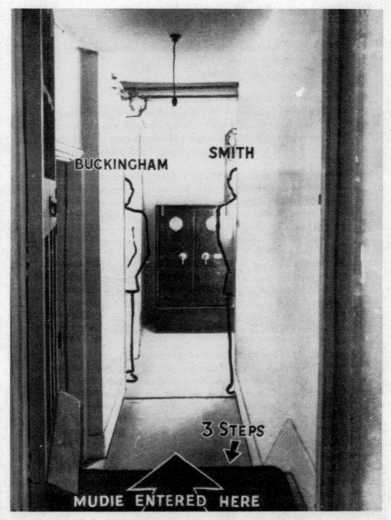

A picture reconstruction of how Mudie was lured to his death

The prosecutor taxed Smith on this point:

'He said, "you're stifling me"?'

'Yes.'

'And did you say the answer he got was, "you are breathing your last"?'

'That was only said in joking form.'

'Tremendously funny, do you think?'

'Well . . .'

'You appear to think it was extremely humorous.'

'No, not extremely humorous. No, it was done to frighten this man.'

Weighing much more heavily against Smith, though, was the fact that the car he hired had been seen at the chalkpit *before* Mudie disappeared. If he was at that time reconnoitring for a suitable grave, it can hardly have been for a living victim.

As for the precise mode of Mudie's death, the experts were in some disagreement. One inclined to the view that he had been subjected to a pretty heavy 'roughing-up'; another that all wounds were trivial apart from the rope-mark around the neck, which suggested that the victim had been suspended by the cord. Speculation along these lines might have been insignificant in themselves, but for the extraordinary testimony of a man named Robert Cruikshank.

He was brought forward by Ley's solicitors. And in a sensational development, he told the court that on the fatal night, he had been trying to burgle Ley's premises. He had found a man trussed up in a chair, and in panic had pulled at the rope. Had he accidentally killed the victim? Cruikshank, it transpired, had a police record, and his statements were widely disbelieved. Was he covering for Ley, hoping for a reward from him? It was doubtful that he was ever at the house.

As for Ley, he denied any knowledge of the conspiracy. He did not doubt that Mudie had been brought to his house, nor that he had been bound there and gagged with a rag which came from the premises. He simply brazened it out, offering no satisfactory alibi for the night of the murder. He blustered and rambled, apparently relying on the lack of direct evidence connecting him personally with the crime. The ex-justice minister had, after all, plotted his vengeance from afar. The jury could take the word of a former minister of state, or of two paltry London working men.

There is always a problem in long-distance plotting, though – the problem of the pay-off. Both Smith and Buckingham testified that Ley had paid them on the night £200 in one-pound notes. Ley's bank records showed that he had made two withdrawals of £250 and £300 shortly beforehand. And the withdrawals were in one-pound notes. Ley stated that the sums were for 'curtain furnishings'. Why not pay by cheque? His suppliers wanted cash, said the defendant. But he

John McMain Mudie

had receipts? No, Ley admitted, he had no receipt for either transaction.

The trial lasted for four days, but the jury took less than an hour to consider its verdict. When they came back into court, they declared both Ley and Smith guilty. Ley formally complained that the judge's summing-up had been biased, but a subsequent appeal failed. Both men were sentenced to be hanged.

The whole case had begun with a head in a noose – but it did not end in that way. Statements made during the trial had revealed a crazed, obsessive element in Ley's jealousy. And while awaiting execution, the ex-justice minister was examined by a Medical Board of Enquiry. It found him to be insane; not just given to jealousy but paranoid in the medical sense. Only three days before he was due to be hanged, a reprieve was granted and Ley was committed instead to Broadmoor.

That decision appeared to leave Smith alone to endure the ultimate penalty for murder. But, in a startling and controversial decision, he was also granted a reprieve. There was no question of the joiner being criminally insane; he had murdered strictly for cash. The Home Secretary's decision can only be explained in very human terms of fair play. Ley was clearly the moving force behind the murder, and Smith was only his instrument. To let the mastermind live and hang his subordinate would have been too dark an irony. The quality of mercy (however illogically applied) offered the only way out of the dilemma.

Lawrence John Smith had his sentence commuted to life imprisonment. And as for Ley, he did not enjoy a long period of grace. Fate dealt him the blow which the Home Secretary had withheld: he died at Broadmoor on 24 July 1947, succumbing to a haemorrhage of the brain.

'Oh, God, I am Not Guilty!'

Writer George Orwell set the scene. It is a peaceful Sunday afternoon in pre-war England. You have enjoyed the roast and the steam pudding, washed down with a cup of mahogany-brown tea. The fire is lit, you put your feet up on the sofa and reach for the Sunday newspapers. 'In these blissful circumstances, what is it that you want to read about? Naturally, about murder.'

CAREFULLY LAID PLANS

For preference, the drama should be one of stealth and unfold against a background of intense respectability. Orwell cites a handful of classics in his *Decline of the English Murder*. There was the affair of Dr Palmer, for example, a Victorian physician who secretly poisoned 14 people. There was Crippen of course. And there was also the case of Thompson and Bywaters.

The domestic setting in suburban Ilford was perfect. Dark, driving passions lurked just beneath the surface. And Edith Thompson's sinister love letters seemed to prove that the crime was one of convenience, coolly arranged at a clandestine meeting beforehand.

And yet it wasn't like that. There were no carefully laid plans. And Edith Thompson's terrible cry rings as chill today as it did when the death sentence was passed upon her: 'I am not guilty; oh, God, I am not guilty!'

Percy and Edith Thompson had lived a largely uneventful life at their home in Ilford, Essex. He was a shipping clerk and she the book-keeper at a firm of wholesale milliners. Married in February 1915, both had their own careers, and the union produced no children. Still, all the neighbours agreed that they seemed a perfectly ordinary couple.

Young Frederick Bywaters came into their lives in the summer of 1921. He was one of a party of people who joined Percy and Edith for an August Bank Holiday on the Isle of Wight. There, he and Edith became mutually attracted, and after the holiday Bywaters lived for a while in the Thompsons' home as a lodger. But Percy grew suspicious: there was a row, and Bywaters quit the household.

Bywaters was only 19 at the time, and worked as a ship's writer on the P. & O. line. Eight years younger than the married woman, he was nonetheless of a strong and domineering temperament. He suggested a divorce, which Percy refused to grant, and the secret liaison continued for some time before the lovers managed to share a bed. Mostly, the affair was restricted to brief meetings in teashops and elsewhere. Because of his job on the S.S. *Morea*, Bywaters was only in England between voyages. And it was during the periods of separation that Edith wrote her fateful letters.

There was a mass of them. When the case came to trial, no fewer than 62 love letters were submitted by the prosecution. It was an extraordinary correspondence: passionate, sinister and utterly compelling.

Edith generally wrote to her lover as 'darlint' (a diminutive of 'darlingest'). And in the missives to her distant paramour she described how she was trying to get rid of her husband by putting poison or ground glass in his food ('big pieces too – not too powdered'). She returned to the theme on several occasions, complaining that her poisoning attempts had aroused Percy's suspicions: 'he puts great stress on the fact of the tea tasting bitter "as if something had been put in it," he says . . . when he was young (he) nearly suffocated by gas fumes. I wish

Frederick Bywaters is arrested at Ilford Station

we had not got electric light, it would be easy. I am going to try the glass again occasionally – when it is safe.'

Additionally, Edith sent her lover newspaper snippets concerning cases of death by poisoning. She hoped that the proposed crime would not affect their relationship: 'This thing that I am going to do for both of us will it ever – at all, make any difference between us, darlint? Do you understand what I mean? Will you ever think any the less of me?'

And she encouraged Bywaters to feel jealous. One passage in particular was to take on special significance: 'Yes, darlint, you are jealous of him – but I want you to be – he has the right by law to all that you have the right to by nature and love – yes, darlint, be jealous, so much so that you will do something desperate.'

All very damning on the surface. Yet the evidence suggests that Edith was playing mind-games: exciting herself with make-believe projects that many an unhappy wife may have entertained from time to time. Above all, she wanted to bond Bywaters to her. He was young, handsome and impetuous. By seeming willing to murder on his behalf, she hoped to secure his affections.

In September 1922, Bywaters returned from a voyage and the secret meetings resumed anew. On the afternoon of 3 October, the couple had a rendezvous in a London teashop. Afterwards, Edith went to the theatre with her husband. As they were walking home together from Ilford station along Belgrave Road, Bywaters sprang out from the shadows.

There was a brief quarrel. Bywaters pulled a knife and stabbed Thompson several times. A witness heard Edith scream: 'Oh, don't! Oh, don't!' The attacker fled back to the shadows as his victim fell, coughing blood, to the pavement.

Immediately, Edith ran for help, rushing until she met a group of people with the words: 'Oh, my God, will you help me, my husband is ill; he is bleeding.' A doctor was called for but arrived too late. Percy was dead, and Edith, now hysterical, sobbed: 'Why did you not come sooner and save him?'

Although Edith did not name the assailant, Bywaters soon fell under suspicion, was tracked down and arrested. Some of the love letters were found in his ship's locker; others were at his mother's home. Of course, they horribly implicated his mistress, and the pair went to trial at the Old Bailey together.

Home Life Of The Italians
Jealousy led a 42-year-old Italian to bite his wife's nose so hard that the wound needed 15 stitches.
    'Latins react differently from the British to domestic troubles', said Mr W.A. Ellis, at Prestatyn.
                                                            News of the World

THE WORLD'S GREATEST CRIMES OF PASSION

Frederick Edward Francis Bywaters was charged with murder, and Edith Jessie Thompson with incitement to the crime.

Thompson confessed to the killing, but claimed not to have intended murder. After he sprang from the darkness, the fatal quarrel allegedly ran as follows:

Bywaters: 'Why don't you get a divorce from your wife, you cad?'

Thompson: 'I've got her, I'll keep her, and I'll shoot you.'

Believing that Thompson was armed, Bywaters pulled a knife in fear of his life: 'I did not intend to kill him. I only meant to injure him. I gave him an opportunity of standing up to me as a man but he wouldn't.' Questioned about the love letters, he stated that it never entered his head that Edith had really tried to poison her husband: 'She had been reading books. She had a vivid way of declaring herself. She would read a book and imagine herself a character in the book.'

The prosecution alleged that the murder had been plotted in the teashop that afternoon. Bywaters repudiated the charge. But, given the mass of compromising material in the love letters, passion and premeditation seemed inextricably linked.

Edith's counsel had tried desperately to keep the damaging correspondence out of the courtroom as inadmissible evidence. The petition failed. The defence also failed in trying to persuade Edith herself to stay out of the witness box. She was not obliged to testify, and doing so only gave the prosecution a chance to cross-examine her about the letters. Edith, however, insisted on facing her accusers, and the damning passages were read out time and again in court.

And what of those sinister extracts? The selections read out in court were all passages chosen by the prosecution. In fact, only a very few refer directly to murder attempts. As in all love letters, the writer had obliquely mentioned all kinds of private secrets. The illicit lovers had considered many different ways out of their love tangle: divorce, elopement and even a suicide pact, for example. Murder was just one of the possibilities they toyed with, and many elusive references to a proposed 'drastic action' or similar were quite capable of a different interpretation.

Edith had penned thousands upon thousands of words, most of them just lover's 'gush'. It was only in the edited version that the correspondence appeared purely murderous. Some of the most apparently sinister passages clearly refer, in their context, to something the defence counsel dared not explain. This was an abortion which Edith was trying to arrange ('I am still willing to dare all and risk all if you are'). The defence obviously felt that it could not afford to be explicit. Enough stigma was attached to adultery; to throw in abortion would make Edith appear more infamous still.

The few direct references to murder attempts were Edith's calamitous fibs. She testified that she made them all up to try and bind Bywaters to her. If the

Bywaters at the inquest

prosecution was to be believed, Percy had been fed an almost daily diet of splintered glass and poison pellets. In fact, the pathologist stated that no trace of poison or of glass was found in Percy Thompson's body.

In effect, the evidence clearly indicates an impulse killing by Edith's lover. Bywaters had not specially armed himself for the encounter; the knife was one which he always kept in his coat pocket (seafarers, facing the hazards of foreign ports, commonly carry a blade). The witnesses' testimony agreed that the attack had dismayed and horrified Edith. She had cried: 'Oh, don't!', she had tried to summon help. 'Oh, God, why did he do it? I didn't want him to do it,' she had sobbed when she first learned that Bywaters had been arrested.

Yet it was as the scheming older woman that she was depicted. Contemporaries have described how, in the witness box, she seemed to exude a heady sexuality which turned the jury against her. The judge was strongly hostile to both prisoners in his summing up, and referred to Edith's 'wicked affection' for her lover. The jury took some two hours to consider its verdict:

Clerk of the Court: Members of the jury, have you agreed upon your verdict?

Foreman of the Jury: We have.

Clerk of the Court: Do you find the prisoner, Frederick Edward Francis Bywaters, guilty or not guilty of the murder of Percy Thompson?

Foreman of the Jury: Guilty, sir.

Clerk of the Court: Do you find the prisoner, Edith Jessie Thompson, guilty or not guilty of the murder of Percy Thompson?

Foreman of the Jury: Guilty.

Asked whether he had anything to say before sentence of death was passed, Bywaters answered: 'I say the verdict of the jury is wrong. Edith Thompson is not guilty. I am no murderer, I am not an assassin.' And when the dread penalty was announced, Edith cried out: '*I am not guilty; oh, God, I am not guilty!*'

An appeal failed. For Edith a petition signed by thousands was submitted to the Home Secretary, but no reprieve was granted. Edith's mother visited her in the condemned cell and asked: 'How could you write such letters?' The submissive mistress replied sadly: 'No one knows what kind of letters he was writing me.'

Bywaters himself protested Edith's innocence to the end. Calmly accepting his own fate he wrote: 'For her to be hanged as a criminal is too awful. She didn't commit the murder. I did. She never planned it. She never knew about it. She is innocent, absolutely innocent. I can't believe they will hang her.'

But they did. Thompson and Bywaters died within moments of each other on the morning of 9 January 1923. Frederick Bywaters faced his end bravely at Pentonville. At Holloway, Edith Thompson had to be carried to the scaffold; she was in a state of collapse as they fitted the noose around her.

The Deadly Apéritif

On Friday 24 August 1973, a registered parcel arrived at the home of Tranquillo Allevi. His wife Renata took it in, as her husband was out at the time. She placed it on his desk, and when he returned, Tranquillo opened it up to find a bottle of apéritif. It was made by a well-known firm of Italian liquor manufacturers, and the accompanying letter invited him to become their local representative in a new sales campaign.

Allevi was a prosperous dairy farmer who lived near San Remo on the north Italian coast. Such invitations were not uncommon, and the 50-year-old dairyman took the bottle to his office where he put it in the fridge. It was a welcome gift, whether he took up the offer or not. Probably he forgot about it in his concern to get on with the day's business.

The bottle remained in the fridge that night and the whole of the following day. It was a Saturday – the day on which, by custom, he would take his wife to dine at the casino restaurant in San Remo. The evening passed pleasantly enough. Having driven Renata home after the meal, Allevi went on to his office to clear up some business. A salesman and another friend joined him there. The night was warm and the trio took off their jackets. Remembering the apéritif, Allevi went to the fridge and returned with the chilled appetizer.

He produced three glasses and poured out the drinks. Raising his glass in a toast, he tossed back its contents in one. The others only sipped – which was lucky for them. For, seconds later, Allevi crumpled to the floor. He was racked with spasms and gasping for breath.

Dismayed, his companions put down their glasses. One phoned the police who came quickly. The three men were rushed to hospital where the two friends were purged with emetics and recovered. Allevi, however, died.

Doctors were quick to diagnose death by poisoning. And in due course it was found that the apéritif contained enough strychnine to kill 500 men.

Who had tampered with the bottle? Enquiries at the manufacturers revealed that although they had sent out some samples with invitations, Allevi was not on their list. His letter followed their customary formula. But it had been typed on a plain sheet, not the company's headed notepaper. It was, moreover, unsigned.

Allevi had no special business rivals. He was generally well enough liked. And suspicion fell initially on Renata, Allevi's grieving wife. She was some 12 years younger than her husband. Enquiries revealed that she had several male admirers outside her marriage: her husband's bookkeeper; an Army officer; and a veterinary surgeon who had treated the dairy herds.

Renata, however, had been visibly distressed at the news of her husband's sudden death. She responded to questioning with every appearance of truthfulness. Far from trying to dissociate herself from the bottle, she herself informed police that she had taken it into the household. She also stated, unprompted, that it was her idea that the apéritif should be taken to the office and placed in the refrigerator to cool.

As investigation proceeded, the police checked up on the movements of her admirers on the fateful day when the parcel was posted. It had been sent from Milan, which seemed to let off two of the suspects. The bookkeeper could prove he had been in San Remo; the Army officer was on duty at the time. That left the veterinary surgeon, Dr Renzo Ferrari.

A suave professional man, Ferrari had been in Milan on the 23rd, renewing his veterinarian's license. Moreover, the police discovered that two days earlier he had bought six grammes of strychnine at a chemist's near his place of work. This was not in itself suspicious – the doctor often bought the substance there for treating sick cattle.

But there was stronger evidence against him. Checking up on typewriters he had access to, detectives discovered a machine at the town hall in Barengo. It appeared to match the typing on the poisonous invitation. Dr Ferrari was a local government officer. He used the town hall in his work.

Ferrari was charged with the murder, and the trial caused a sensation in Italy. This was no hot-blooded Latin-style *crime passionnel*. The defence counsel fiercely challenged the forensic evidence, and there were problems surrounding the precise motive. Ferrari had only recently become engaged to the daughter of a wealthy family. Why should he jeopardise his future? Ferrari claimed that his relationship with Renata was a purely sexual one. He said he was happy to break off the liaison when he met his fiancée.

Renata, dressed in widow's black, told a different story in the box. She testified that it was she who broke off the affair. It happened, she said, when her husband found out that she had been deceiving him. Ferrari refused to accept the breach. She had weakened at first, but then come to a final decision: 'I will not return to you.'

'We'll see,' the veterinarian had replied.

The poison, according to the prosecution, had been inserted by syringe through the cork of the intact bottle. And the final, damning evidence was supplied by a representative of the drinks firm. He stated that although no bottle had been sent from the company to Mr Allevi, one had been dispatched – with an invitation — to Dr Renzo Ferrari.

On 15 May 1974, a panel of judges found the accused guilty of murder with premeditation. The sentence amounted to some 30 years, including consecutive sentences for the attempted murder of Allevi's two drinking companions.

It should be remembered that almost anyone – including Renata – might have sampled the deadly apéritif. This, if anything ever was, was a case of bottled rage.

Otterburn?

Cowering in the lonely farmhouse on the Yorkshire moors, Dorothy Morton and her nurse-companion knew that something was wrong. It was past 3 o'clock in the morning and they were still fully dressed, waiting for Mr Morton's return. He should have been back hours ago from his trip to Oldham where he had gone to buy horses. The groom had been acting strangely all evening, and Mrs Morton had special cause for concern. Ernest Brown, the groom in question, had been her lover and was a violent man consumed with hatred for his employer. The two women heard creaking on the stairs. What was going on? Where was Dorothy's husband?

The creaking ceased. But at 03.30 the crackle of flames could be heard outside. Mrs Morton pulled back the curtain and saw that the garage was ablaze. Hurriedly, she rushed to the telephone to summon help, but as her fingers grasped the receiver no buzzing tone greeted her ears. The line was dead. Someone had cut the wire.

In stark terror, the two women fetched Mrs Morton's child and, with blankets under their arms, they fled from the house. The rest of the night they spent huddled under a hedge watching as the fire raged. In due course, the groom appeared on the scene and rushed to the house, calling, 'Mrs Morton! Mrs Morton!' Neither of the women called out in reply, but stayed in the shadows as he ran to release the startled horses. Some time later, the local fire brigade arrived to try and deal with the conflagration but it was daylight before the blaze was brought under control, and by that time quite a crowd had gathered. One person, though, who never arrived to view the damage was Mr Morton himself. The missing husband had been in the garage all the time – slumped in the passenger seat of the Chrysler saloon from which his charred remnant was eventually recovered.

The Moors' Garage Fire of 1933 came as the climax to a four-year drama. The dead man was Frederick Ellison Morton, prosperous managing director of a firm called Cattle Factors Ltd. His wife, Dorothy, was a beautiful woman with hazel eyes and fine, athletic build. She was especially fond of foxhunting, a pursuit which she enjoyed on the horses her husband kept. It seems that she was not averse to bedroom athletics either. And when in 1929, Ernest Brown was hired as a groom she found that they shared more than an interest in horses. The groom became Mrs Morton's lover, and a triangle took shape.

Ernest Brown was a personable man and a stylish dresser when not in his corduroys. He was by no means ill-educated either. But there was a streak of violence in his nature which soon came to disturb Mrs Morton. At the trial, she was to state that she learned to dislike him, only continuing the liaison through fear. Through threats, Brown forced his attentions on her and she rarely complied willingly.

The Mortons moved to Saxton Grange in the West Riding early in 1933. Mrs Morton had a 2-year-old child, and the nurse-companion, Ann Houseman, lived in. Ernest Brown was put up in quarters of his own – a little wooden cottage not far from the farmhouse. His servile status rankled and, in the jargon of the day, he had 'ideas above his station'. When, one day in June, he was asked to mow the lawns his fierce pride got the better of him. Ernest Brown threw up the job and quit the Morton household.

Mrs Morton's respite from her lover did not last long. Within days, Brown was back at the farm demanding reinstatement. As Mr Morton was away on a business trip, the groom insisted that his wife phone him. He stood over her as she made the call – with his hands about her neck, threatening to strangle her if she failed to persuade her husband.

Ernest Brown was reinstated – but not in his old post of groom. The man who had refused to mow the lawns was taken back only as an odd-job man. This was a bitter humiliation, and afterwards Brown seethed with hatred for Frederick Morton, a vindictive hatred in which jealousy and maimed pride jostled side by side. 'I will clout the little bugger one of these nights', he told a worker at the farm. On another occasion he threatened to ruin Morton's business: 'I can wreck this place and I shall do it.'

Brown nursed his resentment through the summer. And things were made worse when he learned that Dorothy Morton had taken another lover. This man was never identified at the trial, but Mrs Morton admitted his existence. The mystery man was referred to as the 'phantom lover', though his was an all-too fleshly reality.

On 5 September 1933, the tensions snapped. While Frederick Morton was buying horses in Oldham, Brown came into the farmhouse demanding to know what Mrs Morton had been doing that day. She admitted that she had gone bathing with 'Mr X' and this threw him into a fury. During the quarrel, Brown struck Dorothy Morton to the ground. And that evening began the sequence of events which culminated in a night of terror.

At 21.30, Dorothy and the nurse heard gunshot outside, and a hail of pellets rattled at the window. Soon after, they came upon Brown in the kitchen. He claimed to have been shooting at rats. At 21.45, there was a telephone call for Morton, which the nurse answered in the hall. She told the caller that her employer was not there but would soon be back, suggesting he call again at ten. Brown was loitering in the hall for no apparent reason and soon afterwards went into the kitchen to fetch a game knife. The caller did try to ring back at the appointed time – but he never got through. At some time before ten, the line had been cut.

Later, Brown appeared at the farmhouse again with a shotgun in his hand. He told the nurse that he wanted to see Dorothy, but the girl refused to let him meet her mistress alone. Eventually, Brown went away, leaving the two women frightened and anxious in the house.

At 23.30, Mrs Morton and the nurse thought that they heard a car coming. Assuming it was Frederick Morton, they went downstairs to wait for him. But he never turned up. Instead, when they opened the door, they found Brown again who told them, 'The boss has been in and gone out again.'

Gone out again? Brown's sinister prowlings had them seriously disquieted and when it became clear that he did not intend to leave they kept him talking about everyday matters. It was midnight before Brown finally left. There remained the long vigil until 03.30 when sounds of explosion announced the fire.

When help came to the scene of the conflagration, Brown told a bystander, 'By God! If the boss is in there, he will never be seen again.' And later he provided his own version of events for the police. The ex-groom said that Morton had indeed driven back that night, arriving at 23.30, in a drunken state (or 'clever side up'). Brown had left him racing the engine of the Chrysler in the garage where a second car was parked. The fire, he assumed, must have started through the Chrysler backfiring.

A plausible enough theory at first glance. But the police were to discover more sinister features in the case. There was the telephone wire, cut clean through with a knife. There was the emerging story of Brown's liaison with Dorothy. Above all, there was the grim mass of incinerated flesh which had been Frederick Morton.

Practically nothing remained of the managing director. When the gutted Chrysler was withdrawn from the debris, the victim's body could only be identified through two bunches of keys and a unique platinum diamond ring. Amid the charred remains, only one tiny scrap of scorched flesh still survived in recognisable condition. It was a portion from the stomach – and found to be peppered with shotgun pellets. From the concentration of wounds, forensic scientists determined that Morton had been shot at point blank range. He had not died drunk in an accidental fire – he had been murdered before the flames started. As the prosecutor noted when the case came to trial, 'If ever Fate played a murderer a dirty trick, it did so here. Had the wound been in the upper part, it would never have been discovered.'

Brown was the obvious suspect. To the end he protested his innocence, but the evidence against him was overwhelming. Apart from motive and opportunity, bloodstains were discovered on Brown's clothes and shotgun. The clinching detail was the game knife which the ex-groom had taken from the kitchen. From corresponding marks on blade and wire, it was determined that the knife had severed the cord.

The precise time of the murder could not be determined, but the prosecution contended that Brown probably shot his employer as early as 9.30, then concocted the story about 'shooting rats'. He had rained bullets at the window in case either of the two women had heard the sound of gunfire. As for the later sounds of a car arriving, it should be remembered that there were two vehicles in the garage.

The best the defence could do was to try and shift the blame, by implication, to the unnamed 'phantom lover'. The accused was asked, 'Is it your idea that some other lover of Mrs Morton's who disliked her husband shot him and set the place on fire?' Brown replied, 'It may well be.'

But it was a hopeless case. Ernest Brown was found guilty and hanged at Armley Prison, Leeds, on 6 February 1934. The only mystery surrounding the affair derived from the murderer's last words – but a big and tantalizing mystery it turned out to be. When masked and pinioned on the scaffold, Brown was asked by the chaplain if he wanted to make a confession. From beneath the hood, the condemned man's voice uttered three syllables: either 'Ought to burn' or 'Otterburn'.

Did he mean to imply that he ought to burn, as his former employer had burned? Or was he confessing to a sensational unsolved crime committed at Otterburn 100 miles away?

It had been an extraordinary incident – another 'blazing car murder'. In January 1931, 28-year-old Evelyn Foster had been found on a moor in a burning taxi belonging to her father's firm. In her agony, the dying girl described how she had picked up a fare near her Otterburn home. The man was heading for Ponteland, but during the journey he threatened and sexually assaulted her. She claimed he poured fluid over her from a bottle, and having set the vehicle ablaze launched it careering off onto the moor.

Evelyn Foster died of her injuries, the inquest reporting wilful murder. But it was suggested that the girl might have accidentally immolated herself while trying to burn the car for the insurance money. The police, in fact, issued a statement after the inquest, to the effect that no murderer had ever existed.

Were they doing her an injustice? And if so, was Ernest Brown the killer? Evelyn Foster described her assailant as a rather stylish dresser, and said that he had a slight Tyneside accent – details applying to Ernest Brown. The ex-groom was a man of violent temper, not above threatening his mistress to achieve forced intimacy. At the time of the Otterburn incident, he was still a groom in the Morton household, and his job involved travelling about the country to attend horse and cattle sales.

Was he a double murderer? We shall never know. Seconds after uttering his last three syllables Ernest Brown jerked into eternity.

Chapter
Five

Was it murder?

A lovers' tryst is a private affair. But when two victims of flawed passion meet alone – and one of them is shot dead – it becomes an issue of public concern. Some of the most sensational courtroom dramas have followed love tragedies enacted behind closed doors.

Who pulled the trigger when Caesar Young was killed in a hansom cab with his chorus girl? Did Mrs Barney's pistol go off accidentally in the Knightsbridge Mews? And what was the intention of headmistress Mrs Harris when she drove to the fatal rendezvous with the world famous Scarsdale Diet doctor? Did she have suicide in mind? Or was it murder?

Death and the Diet Doctor

His book was a bestseller. When the case came to court it was found that eight out of the twelve women vetted for the jury had followed the Scarsdale Diet. A feeble joke went the rounds when the murder suspect was named: it was said that Mrs Harris had killed Dr Tarnower because she failed to lose weight as promised. And at the autopsy, a fascinating statistic was revealed. Dr Tarnower, 69, 'a moderately well-developed and well-nourished white male,' measured 70 inches tall and weighed 175 lbs. By his own diet plan, the millionaire physician was 15 lbs overweight!

Dr Herman Tarnower ('Hi' to his friends) lived in a fashionable section of New York's Westchester suburb. He helped to found a flourishing clinic at Scarsdale, and there used to recommend a diet programme for his overweight patients. Originally, the plan was no more than two pages long, but in 1979 the doctor published a greatly expanded version under the title of *The Complete Scarsdale Medical Diet*. 'Lose 20 lbs in 14 days', was the book's boast. Besides the initial Basic Plan there were Gourmet, International, Vegetarian and Money-saving variations. Millions followed the diet, and the doctor became world-famous.

Physically fit and active for his age, Tarnower had a taste for the good life. He enjoyed golf, fishing, travel to exotic places – and good eating, too, at the intimate dinner parties he gave at his Westchester home. A bachelor of long standing, Dr Tarnower also enjoyed women.

He had many casual affairs. But for some 14 years, the doctor had pursued a steady liaison with Mrs Jean Harris, headmistress of the highly respectable Madeira Girls' School in Virginia. It was a very 'adult relationship'. Mrs Harris was a divorcee whose own husband had died. She expressed no special jealousy about his philanderings. Nor did she ask for marriage; yet she was hostess at his dinners, the couple shared foreign holidays, and Mrs Harris helped to edit the famous book.

This civilised arrangement was jeopardised, however, when Lynne Tryforos entered the scene. She was the doctor's nurse-secretary at the clinic, an attractive young woman with whom Tarnower began to spend more and more time. In the year before the fatal event, for example, Dr Tarnower took two winter holidays: the first at Palm Beach with the headmistress; the second in Jamaica with the nurse.

Dr Herman Tarnower

THE WORLD'S GREATEST CRIMES OF PASSION

In March 1980, the time of the shooting, Mrs Harris was 56 and Lynne Tryforos only 37. The 'Swinging Diet Doc' as the press was to call him, was trying to jilt his long-standing mistress in favour of a replacement some 20 years younger. Nothing that emerged in the coming case could mask the essential callousness of the doctor's action. It was almost as if he were trading a life rather as he might have traded an old car – for a new model. Public sympathy was heavily in favour of Mrs Harris at the outset of the trial. And for feminists especially, she seemed to embody the whole plight of exploited womanhood.

The trial was one of the longest ever held in the history of New York State. And amid all the courtroom wranglings, some facts were beyond dispute. On Monday 10 March 1980, Mrs Harris drove the 500 miles from Virginia to New York in a blue Chrysler which belonged to the school. She arrived at around 23.00 on a stormy night and let herself into the house. With her she took a .32 calibre Harrington and Richardson revolver, bought some 18 months earlier. Five of its six chambers were loaded – five more rounds were on her person. She entered the doctor's bedroom while he slept, and in the period which followed several shots were fired. The doctor received four bullet wounds from which he died within the hour.

During the fracas, Tarnower's cook heard the buzzer from the bedroom sounding in the kitchen. She rushed and picked up the receiver, heard a shot and much shouting and screaming. The cook woke her husband and called the police as Mrs Harris left the house. A police officer in the neighbourhood drove to the scene and saw the blue Chrysler ahead. Mrs Harris did a U-turn in the road and went back to the house with the police car following behind.

'Hurry up, hurry up! He's been shot,' she said to the officer. Tarnower was crumpled on the bedroom floor when they arrived, his pajamas drenched in blood. He died in hospital.

The statements Mrs Harris made on the fateful night included: 'I've been through so much hell with him, I loved him very much, he slept with every woman he could find, and I had it.' She said she had come to the house with the intention of committing suicide. There had been a struggle with the gun, which went off several times. Asked who had control of the weapon and who did the shooting, she said: 'I don't know . . . I remember holding the gun and shooting him in the hand.'

Mrs Harris was brought to trial on a murder charge. The hearings began in October 1980, by which time the case was already a *cause célèbre*. And it was five weeks before the trial proper began with a full complement of jurors (8 women, 4 men) agreed on by both sides.

Mrs Harris pleaded not guilty, her counsel claiming, 'We don't want special sympathy because she is a woman, because of her age, because she is frail . . .' The defence asked for no mitigation on grounds of temporary insanity or diminished responsibility. Its case rested squarely on the contention that the defendant went to Westchester to take her own life, and the doctor died in a 'tragic accident'.

Formidable obstacles were ranged against this version of events. For example, if suicide was her intention, why did Mrs Harris take a loaded revolver – *and* carry spare rounds on her person? In fact, by a legal nicety, the prosecution was forbidden to mention that she had much more ammunition in the car.

Then there was the struggle itself. How come the doctor sustained four bullet wounds, and Mrs Harris none at all?

The defence marshalled plenty of evidence to show that Mrs Harris had been feeling suicidal. She had been taking drugs (prescribed by Dr Tarnower) to combat depression. She had recently been facing problems at her school. And she had left several farewell notes to friends and colleagues before the fateful night. One said: 'I wish to be immediately cremated and thrown away'. Another included the sad reflection, 'I was a person and no one ever knew.'

Briefly, her own account of events was that she arrived and found Tarnower in bed. 'Jesus,' he had said, 'it's the middle of the night,' and he told her to go away. She asked for a chance to talk for a little while, and he refused. Wandering into the bathroom, Mrs Harris saw a greenish-blue satin négligée (belonging to her rival). She went back into the bedroom and threw it to the floor. Returning to the bathroom she picked up a box of curlers and hurled them at the window. Tarnower came then to the bathroom and hit her across the face; her mouth was bruised when the police found her. She threw another box, and Tarnower hit her again.

Back in the bedroom she sat on the bed, saying 'Hit me again, Hi. Make it hard enough to kill.' Then, unzipping her bag, she took out the gun. 'Never mind,' she said, 'I'll do it myself.'

By her account, Mrs Harris raised the gun to her head, and as she squeezed the trigger he pushed it away. The shot exploded, Tarnower withdrew his hand and it was covered with blood. 'Jesus Christ,' he said. 'Look what you did.'

In a struggle that followed, Tarnower prised the gun off her, pressing the buzzer with his left hand. The gun lay briefly on the bed, Mrs Harris lunged for it and felt what she thought was the muzzle pressing into her abdomen. Again she pulled the trigger; there was a second explosion – and Tarnower fell back.

Now she held the gun to her head and pulled the trigger, but it only clicked. She tried again and a wild shot ricocheted somewhere. She put the gun to her head 'and I shot and I shot and I shot' but the gun just went on clicking. Back in the bathroom she banged the weapon repeatedly against the tub, trying to empty the chambers, planning to reload. In the end the gun just broke.

Tarnower was still conscious and she didn't realise he was dying as she ran out to find help. She was driving to a nearby phone booth when the police car

Mrs Jean Harris on her way to be sentenced

appeared with its flashing lights. Spotting it, she U-turned to lead it back to the house.

Incredibly complex ballistics evidence was heard at the trial, with abstruse talk about ricochet points, in-and-out gunshot wounds and so on. Additionally, it was shown that the police had behaved with some carelessness in handling the material evidence. Suffice to say that four bullet wounds were found in the doctor's body, and Mrs Harris could only remember three shots being fired. This tended to weigh against her. But it was easy to imagine that in the heat of the struggle, more shots might have been fired without murderous intent. Ultimately, the ballistics evidence was inconclusive.

It was in essence a psychological drama. Mrs Harris was something of an enigma even to partisans of her cause. Small, attractive and neatly turned out, she was very composed in the dock. She showed no apparent remorse for the death of her long-standing lover, and even handled the bloodstained sheets without visible emotion. Sometimes she was petulant with the prosecutor; constantly she could be seen forwarding notes to her own defence counsel. Hers was a sharp mind – she looked neither frail, aged nor abandoned. Nor did she look like a victim.

The defence stressed her suicidal weariness, claiming that no vengeful feelings had motivated her as she drove to Westchester that night. There was no hatred for Tarnower in her soul, only a mortal exhaustion. They had never quarrelled before, she quipped in the box, except over the correct use of the subjunctive. But one piece of evidence weighed massively against her version of events. It came to be known as the Scarsdale Letter.

This was a very long and very angry letter mailed by Mrs Harris on the very morning of the fateful day. It was sent to Tarnower by registered post and recovered from the mail. And the text was one long shriek of outrage against the wrongs she had endured.

Mrs Harris claimed in the letter that Tarnower had cut her out of his will in favour of Lynn Tryforos. She called her rival 'a vicious, adulterous psychotic', and a 'self-serving, ignorant slut.' The headmistress charged Lynne with ripping up dresses from her wardrobe at Tarnower's house. She suspected her of stealing her jewellery too, and of making anonymous phone calls.

The whole tone of the letter was ugly, betraying a violent intensity of emotions. Mrs Harris's central demand was that she be allowed to spend April 19th with Tarnower. This was an important occasion at which the doctor was to be honoured. Mrs Harris was determined to attend 'even if the slut comes – indeed, I don't care if she pops naked out of a cake with her tits frosted with chocolate!'

This from the headmistress of the Madeira Girls' School! The letter undermined all the character witnesses who had been brought from the school to the courtroom. But it did much more. It demonstrated unequivocally that jealousy and rage were burning in her soul. In the box the prosecutor had asked: 'Did you ever consider yourself publicly humiliated by the fact that Dr Tarnower was seeing Lynne Tryforos in public?' She had replied 'No'. Yet, in the letter, she had written: 'I have been publicly humiliated again and again and again . . .'

The defence had refused to plead for leniency on the grounds of diminished responsibility. They had decided to go for complete acquittal on the 'tragic accident' theory. And it now seemed with hindsight a downright mistake.

The prosecution described a phone call from the doctor on the fateful morning. 'Goddamit, Jean, stop bothering me', he had said. And this, it was alleged, was the triggering incident which caused her to take the revolver, the many rounds of ammunition, and head the blue Chrysler to Westchester. No doubt she did intend suicide. But she intended to kill the doctor first.

At the end of a trial lasting nearly a year, the jury delivered its verdict. And it agreed with the prosecution. On 24 February 1981, Mrs Harris was found guilty of the murder charge. She displayed no reaction, but two defence lawyers burst into tears when the result was announced. The verdict carried an automatic jail sentence of at least 15 years which was duly delivered by the judge. Standing upright in the dock, Mrs Harris replied with a lengthy statement beginning: 'I want to say that I did not murder Dr Herman Tarnower, that I loved him very much and I never wished him ill, and I am innocent as I stand here . . .'

She was sent to the Bedford Hills Correctional Facility in Westchester. In December 1981, *The Times* reported that Mrs Harris had abandoned the Scarsdale Diet and had gained 30 lb on prison food.

The Terrible Turk

Rejected by the girl he loved, Mr Darsun Yilmaz, a Turk from Damal, resorted to abduction. One night in August 1972 he crept stealthily into the girl's garden. Reaching her bedroom by means of a ladder he threw a blanket over her sleeping form. Then, with his moaning beloved cocooned over his shoulder, the Terrible Turk made his way down to his car and sped off into the night.

Great was his joy as he later wrestled with the blanket and strove to release the lovely contraband. Great was his chagrin when the cloth slipped away to reveal the girl's 91-year-old grandmother.

'There Has Been an Accident . . .'

They called them the Bright Young Things. In the 1920s, the gilded children of London society pursued gaiety with a special kind of frenzy. The horrors of World War One lay in the past; for the future few thoughts were spared. Instead privileged youth grasped feverishly for the here and now: drinking heavily, driving recklessly and making promiscuous love. They danced to jazz, they held fancy dress balls – life was a funfair of glittering silliness. And inevitably it happened that, once in a while, somebody fell off a roundabout.

Elvira Dolores Barney, 27, belonged to the lost generation. The daughter of Sir John and Lady Mullens, she was a conspicuous figure in society: slender, attractive and arrogant. A brief marriage to an older man had ended in quarrels and separation. With her own inheritance and a rich allowance from her parents, the young Mrs Barney returned to the circuit, looking for a good time – and a lover.

She found him in 24-year-old Michael Scott Stephen, one-time dress designer and all-purpose man-about-town. He was something of a gambler who also sponged off rich women. And when the couple set up home at 21 Williams Mews, Knightsbridge, it was Elvira Barney who paid the bills.

The house lay off Lowndes Square, and the couple scandalised the neighbours with their noisy parties. They had equally noisy quarrels too, and it was on the night of 31 May 1932 that one of these proved fatal.

Around midnight, Mrs Barney's doctor received a telephone call. The woman's voice at the other end of the line was near hysterical: 'For God's sake, doctor, come at once. There has been a terrible accident.' Arriving at the mews cottage, the doctor found Stephen lying dead in the upstairs bedroom. He had been shot at close range through the chest. Nearby was a .32 Smith and Wesson revolver, in which two of the chambers were empty.

'He can't be dead,' Mrs Barney was moaning. 'I love him so . . . Let me die, let me die. I will kill myself.'

That, then, was the tableau: Mrs Barney, her dead lover, and the gun. When the police arrived she was still in a state of distress. A detective asked her to accompany him to the station; she struck him, calling out: 'I'll teach you to put me in a cell, you foul swine.' Alternately tearful and imperious, Mrs Barney telephoned her parents, afterwards warning: 'Now you know who my mother is, you will be more careful of what you say.' But when her parents arrived she went

141

quietly to the station. There she made the same statement that she had made to her doctor. It was a version of events from which she never departed.

She said that she and her lover had come back to the mews cottage, half drunk, from a party at the Café de Paris. Stephen declared that he was going to leave her, and she had threatened to kill herself if he did so. She took the gun from under a cushion where it had been hidden; he leaped at her to prevent the suicide. In the struggle which followed, Stephen grabbed the revolver which went off by accident and killed him.

Since Mrs Barney's was the only evidence then available, she was released from custody. Three days later, however, she was formally arrested. The police had been making enquiries in the neighbourhood.

No one could doubt the violent nature of Elvira Barney's romance. Three weeks before Stephen's death, for example, Mrs Hall, a resident, had seen him come to the mews cottage in the early hours of the morning. He was asking for money, but was told by Mrs Barney to go away. He did so, but came back later that night. He was repulsed again, and on that occasion Mrs Barney had looked out of her window, apparently naked, and shouted down, 'Laugh, baby, laugh for the last time!'

Then she had fired a revolver.

The same witness declared that on the fateful night there had been a loud argument in which Mrs Barney had cried out, 'I will shoot you!' before the gun was fired.

Brought to trial at the Old Bailey on a murder charge, Elvira Barney found some formidable forensic experts ranged against her. Sir Bernard Spilsbury, the eminent pathologist, testified that there were no smoke or scorch marks on the dead man's clothes or body. These were generally found when a victim was shot at point blank range. In fact, the angle of the bullet wound implied that Stephen had been shot from a distance of several feet. Moreover, the gunsmith Robert Churchill noted that the Smith and Wesson had a very heavy action – its pull amounting to 14 lbs. It was hard to see how it could have been fired by accident.

Finally, a mysterious bullet hole had been found in the bedroom wall, but no bullet had been recovered from it. If *two* shots had been fired, it made the case for an accident appear doubly improbable.

Defending Elvira Barney, however, was one of the most brilliant advocates of the day. His name was Sir Patrick Hastings, and although a specialist in civil actions he brought an outstanding legal mind to bear on the criminal case. Significantly, Mrs Hall who had first claimed to hear the words, 'I'll shoot *you*,' changed the words at the trial to 'I'll shoot.' This could well carry the implication that Mrs Barney was threatening suicide, not murder. Moreover Hastings had the same witness support the case for a suicide threat. Discussing the earlier shooting incident, Mrs Hall agreed that Stephen and Mrs Barney

Mrs Elvira Barney arriving at her parents' residence in Belgrave Square

Michael Scott Stephen

seemed very friendly on the morning after the 'Laugh, baby, laugh' episode.

'What conversation passed between you and the young man?' asked Hastings.

'I told him to clear off, as he was a perfect nuisance in the mews.'

'What did he reply?'

'He apologised and said he didn't want to leave Mrs Barney because he was afraid that she might kill herself.'

In fact, Hastings was to contend, the shot fired by Mrs Barney three weeks before Stephen died was not aimed after him in the mews. It was the shot which accounted for the mysterious bullet hole in the bedroom wall. Mrs Barney had fired the gun at random, hoping to persuade her lover that her suicide threats were genuine.

Spilsbury's apparently damning forensic evidence was dismissed as theorizing rather than hard fact. As for Robert Churchill's claim that the gun could not have gone off by accident, Hastings had a dramatic answer. Brandishing the revolver before the court, he pulled the trigger repeatedly at the ceiling. It was a gesture accomplished with the utmost panache (although Hastings is said to have later admitted that the effort made his finger sore).

Mrs Barney herself made a more than favourable impression. She spoke in low, dignified tones, her emotion evident but never overstated. She readily admitted that both her marriage and her affair had been unhappy. A tragic figure in the dock, she seemed more ill-fated than ill-intentioned. They had made love, she said, on the fateful night, but it had not been successful: 'He said that he was not pleased with the way things were going and he wanted to go away the next day and not see me at all. That made me very unhappy. He got up from the bed and dressed. I asked him not to leave me and said that if he did I should kill myself.'

'Did he say or do anything then?'

'He got up and took the revolver, saying, "Well, you don't do it with this!"'

There followed the struggle, and the shot.

In his final speech, Hastings meticulously reiterated the thrust of the defence's case. Only Mrs Barney could say what happened on the night of Stephen's death, and she had never departed from her story. In summing up, the judge paid tribute to the power of Sir Patrick's speech, but left the facts for the jury to interpret.

It was a case, *par excellence*, for a jury. The best experts available had given their testimony, the best legal minds had presided in court. But when all was said and done, the outcome had to revolve around a human assessment of the case. Did she do it, or didn't she?

After only one hour and 50 minutes, the jury declared that she didn't.

Elvira Barney's acquittal was greeted with cheers from a large crowd outside the court. A free woman, she went to France to escape the burden of publicity. But it seems that she had not been greatly chastened by the long courtroom ordeal. As chance would have it, Sir Patrick Hastings also crossed the Channel after the trial, for a holiday with his family. While driving from Boulogne he narrowly escaped death when a car coming from behind overtook him on the wrong side of the road. The driver of the car was Mrs Barney.

Socialite, beauty and subject of scandal, Elvira Barney never got a chance to outlive the label of Bright Young Thing. Four years after the trial she was found dead in a Paris hotel bedroom. She was 31 years old.

Sir Patrick Hastings

A Rifle at the Party

The pre-Christmas staff party at New Zealand's Dunedin General Hospital was held on 12 December 1954. Dr John William 'Bill' Saunders, 27-year-old medical officer, took Frances Kearney, a senior student at the hospital. Also present at the party was Dr Florence Whittingham, a house surgeon who had been Saunders' fiancée. She went alone to the party – alone, that is, except for a .303 rifle.

She arrived late. While the party was getting into its swing, Florence Whittingham stayed in her own apartment, writing to a friend a letter that she never in fact posted. Its sentiments were bitter and despondent: 'I can no longer cope and Bill makes things so miserable for me there seems little left. I have so much pain . . .'

She came after midnight, nursing her pain and her rifle. Groups of party-goers had by now crowded into the quarters of one of the hospital surgeons. Florence Whittingham found her former lover in the corridor; and suddenly, above the chatter and the chink of glasses in the living room, voices could be heard raised in anger outside. There was shouting and screaming – a shot detonated – and the guests rushed out into the corridor.

For a moment the scene was frozen, as in some nightmarish tableau. Dr Saunders was kneeling, blood-spattered, on the floor. Florence Whittingham stood before him and, as the wounded man swayed on his knees, she lent forward to embrace him. She was babbling hysterically: 'Bill, listen to me, Bill.' But the medical officer heard nothing as he slid dying from her arms. No-one called for a doctor – the apartment was crowded with medics. But all of their expertise counted for nothing in the case of Dr Saunders. He was dead before the stretcher arrived.

The case stunned New Zealand. Explosions of love and despair were not expected in the sober professional community of Dunedin, the South Island seaport founded by Scottish Presbyterians. And although clearly a crime of passion, the affair had its perplexing features too. A rifle is no natural choice of weapon for suicide. Did Dr Whittingham go to the party intending murder or, as she claimed, something else?

Dr Senga Florence Whittingham was 27 at the time; the same age as her former fiancé. And no-one could deny that she had cause for grievance in the events leading up to the tragedy. She had taken up the post of house surgeon at Dunedin early in 1953, and her duties involved working closely with Dr Saunders. Soon they formed a relationship which extended out of hours. As early as May 1953, the medical officer asked Florence to marry him and she was only too happy to accept. In June, the couple went to see Saunders' mother and announced their engagement. They hoped for an early wedding, for Florence was expecting a baby.

Mrs Saunders had her reservations. It had been a lightning romance, and both had their careers to think about. Mrs Saunders advised a period of reflection. They should not get married only for the baby's sake. If necessary, she declared, she would adopt it.

In the event, there was no quick wedding – indeed, no wedding at all. After that meeting with Mrs Saunders, the couple still went on seeing one another. But it seemed to Florence that Bill's ardour had cooled. She sensed that he no longer wanted the baby. When asked about his feelings, Bill denied that he was falling out of love, but he was evasive about the future.

That summer, Florence Whittingham procured an abortion. She knew immediately afterwards that a bond had been broken. Bill was clearly relieved, and in September, with no pressing reason for the marriage to go ahead, he broke off the engagement.

Florence was in despair. Even in the most supportive environment, an abortion may leave deep emotional scars. Had the child been truly 'unwanted' the loss might have been easier to bear. But this baby had been joyfully anticipated – by Florence, at least – as the fruit of love and in the promise of a shared future. She still loved Dr Saunders, still urgently wanted to marry him. But far from easing the relationship, her sacrifice had left her bereft of her lover too. For Dr Saunders, breaking the engagement recalled a more carefree way of living. Once again he became Dunedin's popular – and very eligible – bachelor medical officer.

It was when the bitter realisation of her double-loss dawned that Florence Whittingham bought the .303 rifle. She told a friend who once noticed the gun in her rooms that it was for her brother. In fact, Dr Whittingham had no brother. But if a sudden urge to violence provoked the purchase it seems to have faded away. She took no immediate action, enduring instead long months of waiting and of faint hope. Perhaps Saunders' love would quicken again?

It never did. Through all of 1954, Florence Whittingham was prey to black depression which eroded her vitality. She became a wraith in the corridors of the General Hospital, attending as capably as ever to her patients, but inwardly broken in spirit. Her health was affected and she underwent a major operation. To combat her loss of vitality, she began taking insulin, a drug normally prescribed for diabetics. It proved no cure, though, for lovesickness.

The affair was over, and no amount of pleading could bring Dr Saunders back. Yet she still saw him practically daily in the hospital, confident, ambitious and relishing his restored bachelorhood. What provoked the climax was a trivial enough event. Florence Whittingham learned that her ex-lover would be taking Miss Kearney to the staff party at Christmas. A sense of outrage seems to have seized Florence, for she phoned her rival and in a near-shriek declared, 'This is the mother of Bill Saunders' child speaking!' No doubt a pent flood of recrimination was at her lips, but she got no chance to release it. When Miss Kearney identified the caller's voice as Dr Whittingham's she prudently hung up.

Florence Whittingham was shut out now; shut out of her lover's life and his future. And it was in a mood of total frustration and despair that she had recourse to the rifle.

In the letter she wrote to her friend before taking the gun to the party, Dr Whittingham began: 'I should like you to be of special comfort to my mother and Bill's mother.' By implication, she was considering some kind of dramatic action if 'special comfort' would be required. But the rest of the text expressed, in broken paragraphs, only misery: 'I have had a year of hell . . . I love him but my pleadings are useless.' There was no specific threat.

After the sensational shooting at the party, she was to say quietly, 'It's the first time I've been at peace for a year.' And later: 'I loved him – I couldn't stop loving him. I wanted to frighten him. That's all. Just to frighten him. I didn't mean to shoot him. Just frighten him. That's all.'

When a crime is committed in a state of high emotion, the word 'intention' becomes opaque. Dr Whittingham was brought to trial for wilful murder in February 1955, and the prosecution had a formidable case. The accused had, after all, taken a loaded rifle to the party. The letter she had written was shown in evidence. A ballistics expert, moreover, testified that the .303 could not easily be fired by chance.

In defence, Florence Whittingham's counsel contended that she had pointed the gun at Saunders only as a threatening gesture; the discharge was accidental. Obviously there was great sympathy for the accused when the story of her abortion and operation was made known. But assessing her precise intention at the moment of discharge called for careful consideration. At the end of the six-day trial, the jury deliberated over its verdict for more than seven hours. Returning to the crowded courtroom, the members found Dr Whittingham guilty of manslaughter, but added a strong recommendation to mercy on the grounds that the rifle was fired accidentally. She received a three-year sentence.

In retrospect, the case is as hard to assess as it was in the Supreme Court Building. But the verdict was a fair one. However the gun went off, its purpose at the party was not to destroy a life. It was brought to shock the victim into recognition of wronged love and misery endured. Behind the echo of gunshot, a voice was calling, 'Bill, listen to me, Bill. *Listen* to me.' It was the voice of love locked out.

'I am a Lady'

In March 1914, as war clouds gathered over Europe, a public scandal shook France to its roots. It was a shooting incident – an *affaire d'honneur* – which swept all other issues from the front pages. Even the assassination of the Archduke Franz Ferdinand at Sarajevo was given lesser prominence in the press. That obscure event in Bosnia was to usher in the holocaust of World War One but its significance was not at first grasped. France's Caillaux Affair, in contrast, was reported worldwide and followed with complete fascination.

It did not conform to the classic pattern of a crime of passion, but had all the elements associated with one. There were the tangled emotions of a love triangle, and shots fired by an outraged wife. The victim, though, was the newspaper editor who brought the affair to light.

Gaston Calmette, editor of *Le Figaro*, was the most influential journalist in France. For months he had used the power of his paper to direct a campaign against Henri Caillaux, Finance Minister. The attacks came daily in the form of lampoons as well as bitter textual denunciations. What provoked the editor's wrath was Caillaux's pacificism and – more serious – supposedly treasonable contacts with Germany.

Things came to a head when the editor resorted to personal smears. On the morning of 16 March 1914, *Le Figaro* published a compromising love letter from Caillaux on its front page. The letter was one of several written by the Minister during the period of his first marriage. They were addressed to Henriette, the society beauty who became his second wife. Caillaux's first wife had acquired some of the correspondence and had used it to obtain a hefty cash settlement after the divorce. The business was over, it was a private affair – but reflected no credit on the Minister.

It was the second Madame Caillaux who took action. When the letter was published Henriette could not find her husband, and so headed straight for a gunsmith. In the shop, having tested a Smith and Wesson, she judiciously opted for a Browning automatic. Then she went round to the offices of *Le Figaro* where she shot the editor dead with five bullets. As nervous staff sought to apprehend the killer, Madame Caillaux replied magisterially, 'Let me go. I am a lady. I am Madame Caillaux. I have my car waiting to take me to the police station.'

The Minister was forced to resign, and his wife was brought to trial at the Assize Court of the Seine in July 1914. She faced the charge of murder amid a national furore. Initially, at least, the dead man was presented as a patriot gunned down by a traitor's wife. The courtroom turned into a political theatre of war, in which charges and counter-charges were fired like mortar shells from the entrenched ranks of the rival counsels. In the end, the Caillauxs emerged the political victors, bringing evidence to show that Calmette himself had been involved in unpatriotic propaganda.

But what of the murder charge? Incredibly, Madame Caillaux declared herself innocent of the crime, on the grounds that the gun went off by accident. After the first chance shot, she contended, the rest of the bullets simply streamed out automatically. She gave evidence in the dock with a stately calm and with every appearance of truthfulness. The jury came to the unanimous verdict that Madame Caillaux was not guilty – and she walked from the court a free woman.

Two Cab Mysteries

When one of two lovers gets shot in a sealed cab, the event may be problematic for the law. Should the victim die, the case is likely to rest on the testimony of the survivor. The two stories that follow were different in outcome, yet they shared many features in common. Both shootings, for example, tragically concluded love affairs which were supposedly over already. Both also involved ladies of the stage and took place during the champagne years before the outbreak of World War One.

The first drama was played out in New York, 1904, where Mrs 'Caesar' Young had had enough. Everyone knew about her husband's affair with Nan Patterson, 22-year-old chorus girl from the hit musical *Floradora*. Mrs Young had thwarted one attempted elopement, and now booked passages for her husband and herself on a transatlantic steamer. Maybe a holiday in England would provide a chance of a reconciliation, in which memories of the chorus girl would fade from his mind.

Francis 'Caesar' Young, New York gambler and prominent man of the turf, agreed to the vacation. The passages were booked for 4 June 1904, but on the day before the ship was due to leave, Caesar Young spent a long time with Nan Patterson. The bonds that had united them could not easily be severed: he drank, they argued, and on the morning of the sailing he was again in Nan's company. The couple shared a hansom cab which led along Broadway to a theatreland sensation – and an amazing triple series of trials.

Exactly what happened in the cab? One shot detonated in the vehicle and a passer-by heard Nan cry out, 'Look at me, Frank. Why did you do it?' First, the chorus girl told the driver to make for a nearby drugstore, then to hurry on to a hospital. But it was too late. When the cab doors were opened, Caesar Young was already dead, slumped in the lap of his mistress. His shirt was stained with blood from the bullet-wound in his chest, and the pistol was found in his coat pocket.

Nan Patterson was arrested and charged with murder. If a verdict of guilty was reached, she would go to the electric chair, a device used in New York from 1890, when it had been applied for the first time in the world.

Nan's case first came to court in November 1904, but a mistrial was announced before she could give evidence: one of the jurors had died. At trial two, held the following month, the jury could not agree on a verdict. At the third trial, held in April 1905, the jury was again unable to come to a majority decision.

Throughout her ordeal, Nan had fervently protested her innocence and public opinion was firmly on her side. Ten days after the last trial was concluded, the judge granted a motion that she be discharged. Outside the court, a delirious crowd cheered her to freedom, and in the playgrounds little children were heard to chant:

> Nan is free, Nan is free,
> She escaped the electric chair,
> Now she's out in the open air!

The second cab mystery occurred in the City of London, two years after Broadway's incident. At midnight on Saturday 28 September 1912, the driver of a taxi moving along Fenchurch Street heard three loud bangs behind him. Assuming his tyres had burst, the driver got out to examine the vehicle's wheels. A police constable on night duty also heard the reports and came up to find out what was going on. The tyres were firm and the driver opened the cab door to see if his two passengers were all right. Immediately, a woman toppled headlong out, moaning, 'Mind, cabby, he has a revolver. He has shot me. Drive me to a hospital.'

No sooner were the words uttered than two more deafening reports were heard. Inside the taxi, her companion had tried to shoot himself – blood was spattered all around. The driver rushed his cab with its freight of wounded fares to Guy's Hospital where the woman died within minutes of arrival from wounds to her head and chest. The man, though bleeding severely from head and hands, was saved from death. His name was Edward Hopwood, a failed company director. The dead woman was Florence Alice Silles, stage-name 'Flo Dudley', a music-hall comedienne.

Edward Hopwood was a short man – short of stature and short of funds.

Though married with children, he lived apart from his wife and was practically bankrupt when he first met Flo Dudley. The pair quickly became lovers and must have made a slightly improbable couple for she was statuesque and ample-bosomed, with the full-blown figure so admired in the period. Despite his dire financial straits and his matrimonial state, Hopwood proposed marriage to Florence. She was a widow at 34 and, having no idea that Edward had other commitments, readily accepted. Being a strict Catholic she insisted that they see a priest, to which her lover consented. She also brought Hopwood home to Ilford to meet the sister with whom she shared a house. He was introduced as her betrothed.

Florence's intended, though, seemed curiously evasive about naming the day. He offered a registry office wedding but even the would-be bigamist clearly baulked at the idea of a formal Catholic service. In August 1912, five months after the affair began, Florence would endure no further delay and broke the relationship off. She would have no more to do with the diminutive company director.

Edward grew jealous. He knew Florence was friendly with a man living in Southampton and desiring one last rendezvous, Hopwood resorted to subterfuge. He went to Southampton and, using the other man's name, wired Florence to meet him for dinner at the Holbourn Restaurant for dinner on the night of 28 September.

It was the night of the fatal shooting. That Saturday morning, Hopwood bought an automatic revolver. In the afternoon, he made out his will and wrote a suicide note. At night he made his surprise appearance at the Holbourn Restaurant. Shortly before midnight, the couple hired a cab to go to Fenchurch Street Station. It was during the course of this short trip that the three shots rang out.

Edward Hopwood was tried for murder in December 1912. He refused legal aid, preferring instead to present his own case before the jury. Hopwood's contention was that he pulled out the gun intending suicide, but Florence grabbed him as he produced the revolver. The gun fired accidentally in one rapid burst of three shots.

The judge was by no means unsympathetic. But the prosecution brought forward a forensic scientist who testified that Florence's head wounds could not have been caused by chance. At one point during his final address to the jury, the accused was overcome with emotion and broke into a fit of sobbing. Eventually, when prompted by the judge to continue, Hopwood wept, 'I can say no more.'

There was no triple trial for Edward Hopwood. The jury found him guilty of wilful murder, and sentence of death was passed. Late in December, only three months after doctors at Guy's Hospital had saved Hopwood's life, the hangman took it back at Pentonville.

The Lost Flyer

On Saturday 15 April 1933, *The Times* reported:

> No news has been received of Captain Lancaster, who was flying from
> England to the Cape, since Wednesday. Our Algiers Correspondent
> reports that he left Reggan, an oasis in the Sahara, at half past six on the
> evening of that day for Gao, on the Niger. Sandstorms were causing
> bad visibility. A motor car was sent yesterday by the Trans-Saharan
> Company to search for him.

The celebrated airman had left England at 05.38 on the morning of 11 April,
in an attempt to beat the record for a flight to the Cape. He had reached Oran at
21.00 that night and taken a brief rest there before setting out across the Sahara
desert.

The following day he drifted off course because of heavy sandstorms.
Nevertheless, he managed to reach Reggan where he rested for three hours,
worn out. There was no moon, and a strong northwest wind was blowing. The
local head of the Trans-Saharan Company told him it was madness to take off
when he would not be able to see the day beacons on the main desert motor
track. Lancaster did not even have lighting on his instrument board, for steering
a compass course.

But Lancaster was determined to go. As for lighting, he said, he would
manage with matches and a borrowed pocket torch. Witnesses saw him make a
very bad take-off before vanishing into the evening sky. It was 18.30 on 12th
April. He was not seen alive again.

Was he prompted to make the fatal flight by that reckless spirit shared by all
the pioneer aviators? Or was something else on his mind, urging him to risk the
treachery of the desert? Captain Lancaster had hit the headlines less than a year
before, for something very different. At Miami in August 1932, he had been
brought to trial on a charge of murder.

William Newton Lancaster had served in the RAF during World War One.
He subsequently married and left the Air Force to make a name for himself as a
long-distance flyer. The twenties was the decade of Lindbergh, Cobham and
Kingsford Smith – men who opened up the world's air routes. Women, too,
played their part in those pioneer years, and one of them was Australia's Mrs
Keith 'Chubbie' Miller.

In 1927, Lancaster and Mrs Miller flew as partners in a record-breaking flight

Captain Lancaster and Mrs Miller set off on their record-breaking flight which covered the 13,000 miles from London to Australia. And although both were married they continued to fly as a team, becoming lovers on the ground as well as partners in the air. After their record-breaking flight to Australia, the couple did most of their flying in the United States, and it was there that their tragedy was enacted.

While Lancaster was in Mexico for a spell, Chubbie developed a liaison with American writer Charles Haden Clarke. The pair fell in love and wrote to Lancaster of their plans for marriage. Lancaster returned to Florida with a revolver and confronted the lovers at Mrs Miller's house. There followed a quarrel which ended when the three actors in the drama retired to their respective beds.

During that night, Chubbie was wakened by Lancaster who told her that Clarke had shot himself. The writer was slumped in his room with a pistol lying on the bed. Blood seeped from the head wound from which he later died. Lying by the dying man were typed suicide notes – written on Lancaster's machine.

The death occurred on 21 April 1932. On 2 August of that year, Captain W.N. Lancaster was brought to trial for murder. Much of the 16-day courtroom case revolved around the nature of the fatal wound. Forensic experts debated the possibilities of suicide and murder, while the character of the two men was discussed. According to Chubbie, Clarke had called Lancaster 'one of the finest men he knew.' The defence intended to support the case for suicide by bringing forward a doctor who, after post mortem examination, declared the dead man to be a drug addict. The doctor was sick at the time of the trial, and a motion for adjournment was denied. Nevertheless, after deliberating for six hours, the jury found Lancaster not guilty.

Chubbie had stood by the airman at his trial, but their relationship had inevitably suffered. Though both returned to England, Lancaster's record-breaking attempt of 1933 was a solo flight, made in the 100 h.p. *Southern Cross Minor* – a single-seater plane.

When the plane went missing over the Sahara, search parties were called out. But within ten days of the disappearance, the experts were acknowledging there was very little hope indeed of ever finding the missing aviator alive. In fact, the pilot was not to be found in any condition at all – until more than 29 years later.

In February 1962, a French desert patrol came upon the wreckage of Lancaster's Avro-Avian. The remains of the missing flyer were found beside the debris. His log-book contained entries for eight days after the crash – eight days awaiting death in the desert, in which he recorded his love for Chubbie Miller. Curiously enough, the last entry was made exactly one year to the day after Charles Haden Clarke's death.

What Kind of Murder?

It happened the wrong way round. When a husband comes home to find his wife with another man, it is the husband who traditionally resorts to violence. But the case of Melvyn and Lorraine Clark was rather different . . .

Melvyn Clark was an electronics engineer who lived with his wife and three children in a suburb of Boston. And beneath the surface of domestic content, there lurked illicit passions. When Melvyn was away from home, Lorraine used to attend wife-swapping parties. The partners were selected 'blind': men threw down keys, and the women picked them up without knowing whose bedroom they would be sharing.

Melvyn knew nothing of these frolics. On 10 April 1954, the engineer returned to his home unexpectedly to find Lorraine with another man. The interloper made his excuses and left. A quarrel broke out in the Clark household, during which Lorraine stabbed her husband with a darning needle. Then she shot him dead with two bullets from a revolver.

Afterwards, Lorraine trussed up her husband with wire and lugged his body into the car. She drove to a nearby river and, on the bridge, fixed weights to his legs and heaved him over the edge.

The body was discovered six weeks later, and during interrogation Lorraine confessed to the murder. But what kind of murder was it? Under United States law, first degree murder is deliberate and premeditated, designed to effect a death. Second degree murder is a killing in which deliberation and premeditation are missing. In Lorraine's case, the stab of the darning needle may well have been impulsive. But the two subsequent revolver shots . . .?

In a decision which aroused controversy, her plea of guilty to second degree murder was accepted, and she received a sentence of life imprisonment.

Chapter Six

Whodunit?

A church minister and his choir singer mistress are gunned down in a lover's lane. A womanizing whist expert is shot dead in his locked home by an assailant who mysteriously vanishes. A romantic songwriter and her handyman lover make rival confessions to the same murder.

In these and other cases described, crimes of passion were proven or strongly suspected. The tormenting question for courts and public alike was one beloved of all crime aficionados: whodunit?

Reverend Babykins and His Gay Gipsy

On Saturday 16 September 1922, an adultery was exposed at a lover's lane in New Brunswick, New Jersey. The Reverend Edward Wheeler Hall, Rector of St John's Episcopal Church, was found lying under a crab apple-tree with Mrs Eleanor Mills, the sexton's wife. He was 41 and balding; she a petite 34-year-old. And the couple never got a chance to defend or explain their activities. For they were found dead – murdered at their rendezvous, their bodies scattered with their torn-up love letters.

The pastor's head had been pierced by a single bullet; a bloodsoaked Panama hat lay over his face. Eleanor Mills had been shot three times; her throat, moreover, had been slashed. And as for the love letters, they told in the clearest possible terms of the special relationship which had existed between the minister and the soprano who had sung in his choir.

The letters strewn all around had been written by Eleanor Mills. Scribbled in pencil, they bore witness to intense emotions: 'I know there are girls with more shapely bodies,' the sexton's wife had written, 'but I do not care what they have. I have the greatest of all blessings, the deep, true and eternal love of a noble man. My heart is his, my life is his, all I have is his, poor as my body is, scrawny as they say my skin may be, but I am his forever.'

Someone had emptied the minister's pockets, and his gold watch had been stolen. But mere theft could not have been the motive for the killing. Propped against the dead man's foot was one of his own visiting cards, as if advertising his identity. Whoever shot the lovers had also arranged their bodies side by side in a grotesque embrace. Special savagery had been reserved for Eleanor Mills; not only had her throat been slashed but her tongue and vocal cords had been cut out. With the confetti of love letters playing about the bodies, everything pointed to a crime of passion.

The police interviewed the dead clergyman's wife, Frances Hall. A plain, grey-haired woman nine years older than her husband, she professed complete ignorance of the liaison between her husband and his chorister. All she knew was that on the evening of Thursday 14th, her husband had received a phone call and left the house. He did not come back that night. And although it was a whole day and another night before the bodies were discovered, Mrs Hall at no stage called the police.

James Mills, husband of the dead woman, came up with a strikingly similar story. His wife had not come home on Thursday evening, but he too failed to call the police. When pressed, he said that he thought his wife might have been round at her sister's house. Like Frances Hall, he claimed to know nothing of the secret love affair.

There were many in the pastor's congregation who were not so blinkered. Rumours of the affair had been circulating in New Brunswick long before the murders took place. Perhaps one, or both, of the spouses did know of the liaison, and failed to call the police suspecting an elopement? Speculation along these lines led nowhere.

With the lack of concrete evidence, public interest in the case began to flag. But while a blameless suspect named Hayes was under investigation, a witness turned up – a colourful middle-aged Mrs Jane Gibson who came to be known as the Pig Woman.

Mrs Gibson kept pigs on a smallholding, and claimed to have seen the murder occur on the Thursday evening. Hearing noises that night, and suspecting thieves, she had mounted her mule and gone down the lane. Four figures were arguing under the crab apple-tree: two men and two women. One of these was a white-haired lady, and another a kinky-haired man. There were shouts of 'Don't, don't, don't.' Something glinted in the moonlight. Four shots rang out – and the Pig Woman fled the scene.

When questioned by the police, the Pig Woman identified Mrs Hall as the white-haired woman, and her brother Willie Stevens as the kinky-haired man.

Could the testimony be believed? The case came alive again, and the new evidence coincided with the publication of a batch of letters between Eleanor Mills and the late minister. They were all that a sensation-seeking public could have wished.

To the pastor, for example, Mrs Mills had written: 'I am on my knees, darling, looking up at my noble man, worshipping, adoring . . . I want you – your arms to hold me and hold me close if only to forget this pain for a minute. Dearest, give me some words of comfort.'

In reply, the clergyman had penned a note arranging a tryst for the following day: 'My dearest, my treasure, my anchor, my rock – oh, how I did want to fly off with you this afternoon – I wanted to get away to dreamland – heaven-land – everything seemed so sordid, earthy, commonplace . . . Dearest – love me hard, hard – harder than ever, for your Babykins is longing for his mother.'

Earthbound in New Brunswick, the clandestine lovers had allowed their fancies to roam in an illicit paradise where truth, nobility and wonder, crystal eyes and crushing embraces, were all yearned for with equal intensity. Eleanor was the pastor's 'gay gipsy' and, 'when my arrow enters your haven I am transported to ecstasy,' wrote the stalwart.

And where had this new correspondence come from? The cache of letters was sold to the press for $500 by James Mills. The transaction of course cast considerable doubt on the sexton's claim to know nothing of his wife's affair.

A grand jury was convened in November to assess the case. But the inquiry led to no indictment. For four years the case was as if frozen, neither formally closed nor under active investigation. What broke the ice was a bombshell lobbed from within the late pastor's household.

Louise Geist, who had served the Halls as a maid, got involved in a lawsuit for marriage annulment. Her husband claimed that Louise had been bribed to keep silent before the grand jury: she had in fact accompanied Mrs Hall and her two brothers to the scene of the crime and been a witness to – or a participant in – the vile deeds.

Back to the front pages came the Crab Apple-tree murder. Back to the limelight came James Mills, the Pig Woman and the rest. And into the dock went the clergyman's wife, with her brothers Willie and Henry Stevens.

The trial was held at Somerville, New Jersey, in November 1926. And it seemed at last that the solution was clear. But was it? Actually, Louise Geist repudiated her husband's claims, still insisting she knew nothing of the murder. The Pig Woman was readier than ever to point the finger at Mrs Hall and her brothers, but the hog-farming witness was now dying of cancer. She had to be brought into court on a stretcher, and her aged mother confounded everyone by constantly interrupting: 'She's a liar, a liar, a liar! That's what she is, and what she's always been.'

James Mills, meanwhile, was fiercely cross-questioned and now candidly admitted that he had known all about the affair between his wife and the clergyman. He had read the love letters and, it seemed, had quarrelled bitterly with his wife about the liaison.

Maybe Mills did it? Maybe the Pig Woman did it! (This suggestion was actually made by the defence counsel.)

At the end of the long, confused trial the jury retired for five hours. When they returned, it was with a verdict of not guilty.

Mrs Hall and her brothers were discharged, the pastor's widow becoming a recluse and dying in 1942. The whole affair had scandalised America, and remains one of crime's great unsolved mysteries. One plausible theory has been put forward by William Kunstler in his *The Minister and the Choir Singer* (1964). He suggests that the Ku Klux Klan engineered the double murder as retribution for the couple's violation of Bible teaching on adultery. Certainly, the disposition of the bodies and the mutilation of the errant choir singer suggest ritual elements in the crime. But the theory remains pure conjecture. All that can be said with certainty of the affair is that the love between Edward Hall and Eleanor Mills was true love lived in a morass of deception. And that the lovers paid a terrible price for their idyll in heaven-land.

Whose Hand On the Mallet?

In a conventional whodunit you might expect to find a host of different suspects. But the Rattenbury case of 1935 had a very limited cast. There was Mrs Alma Rattenbury, 38, a writer of popular songs. There was her lover, George Stoner, a chauffeur-handyman barely 18 years of age. And there was 67-year-old Francis Rattenbury, the brutally murdered husband.

The distinguished architect was found battered to death in his favourite armchair. His hair was matted with blood, and there were bloodstains too on the carpet. Rattenbury had been clubbed with a mallet by three heavy blows struck from behind. The question which tormented the public concerned who had wielded the weapon.

Mrs Rattenbury? Her lover? Or had the pair connived at the murder together?

When Alma married Francis Rattenbury in 1925, some comment was made about the disparity between their ages. She was an attractive young woman of great musical talent who had been awarded the *Croix de Guerre* for her services as a nurse in World War One. He in contrast was already middle-aged, a solitary and rather morose man. Rattenbury had, however, won fame and fortune for his architectural designs (his parliament buildings at Victoria B.C. still stand). Alma had no money to speak of.

Yet for ten years their union was happy enough. Not long after the wedding, the couple retired to the Villa Madeira, a pleasant residence in the quietness of Bournemouth. Alma had a son by a previous marriage who came to visit them at holiday time. Rattenbury too had had children by his first wife. And now Alma bore the architect a new son named John. On the whole, the Rattenburys' was an affectionate ménage, in which such tensions as existed hinted little at the coming tragedy.

'Ratz', as his wife called him, was still prone to his fits of melancholy. Sometimes in the evenings he drank rather too much whisky; sometimes he talked morbidly of suicide. But Alma usually restored his spirits, and to occupy her days she took to writing popular songs. She won considerable success in this field, under the name of 'Lozanne'. Her music was published, broadcast and recorded, the most popular of her discs being *Dark-Haired Marie*:

Are you waiting in your garden
By the deep wide azure sea?

THE WORLD'S GREATEST CRIMES OF PASSION

Are you waiting for your loveship,
Dark-Haired Marie?

I shall come to claim you someday,
In my arms at last you'll be,
I shall kiss your lips and love you,
Dark-Haired Marie.

The lyrics, like many of Alma's, evoke a troubled and sensual yearning which is not hard to understand. After the birth of their son John, she and her husband no longer slept together: they had their own separate bedrooms. Rattenbury told her she could 'lead her own life', and perhaps there were many evenings when the Dark-Haired Marie of the Villa Madeira dreamed of the loveship that would come to claim her. It arrived in the form of George Percy Stoner, hired as a chauffeur in September 1934.

He gave his age as 22; in reality he was not yet 18. The affable, good-looking son of a local bricklayer, Stoner was soon driving Alma to the London shops, theatres and cinemas. By the end of November, she and Stoner were lovers, and the young man had moved in to the Villa. It was not a big house. His room was just across the landing from hers.

They quarrelled sometimes. Stoner was an inexperienced young man who clearly felt the need to assert his masculinity before the woman who was old enough to be his mother. He told her to give up drinking cocktails, for example, as they were bad for her. Alma agreed. He used to carry a knife with him and on one occasion threatened to kill her; on another he expressed the urge to take his own life. Perhaps the older woman derived some dark excitement from these adolescent theatricals. But she knew her responsibilities. When he confessed his real age, Mrs Rattenbury tried unsuccessfully to break off the relationship. And when Stoner hinted to her that he was taking drugs, she became worried for her children. Alma confessed the whole affair to the family doctor, and asked him to warn the youth off drug-taking, which Dr O'Donnell duly did.

The affair continued into the spring of 1935. In March 1935, the couple took rooms at a Kensington hotel, posing as brother and sister. They went on a shopping spree in which Mrs Rattenbury bought for her lover a suit, shirts, shoes and silk pyjamas. She even bought him a ring which, humiliatingly, he then presented to her as a token of his love. It was on the day after their return to Bournemouth that the tragedy occurred.

On Sunday 24 March, 'Ratz' was in one of his moods. At teatime he read aloud passages from a novel in which the hero contemplates suicide. Alma only managed to brighten his spirits by suggesting that they take a trip to Bridport the next day, and stay there that night. Rattenbury had a friend and business

Mrs Rattenbury accompanied by her doctor

THE WORLD'S GREATEST CRIMES OF PASSION

Right: the rear of the Villa Madeira in Bournemouth

Below: the constable called to the scene of the suicide takes Mrs Rattenbury's umbrella and handbag to the court

colleague at Bridport, called Mr Jenks. The architect was worried at the time about raising finances for a block of flats. Jenks could help him out in this respect.

The Bridport trip was duly arranged, and the couple played cards that night. At exactly 21.30, Alma went up to bed while her husband returned to his armchair and his novel. Ironically, the book was found folded the next day at a passage where the hero meditates on the problems faced by elderly men who marry younger women . . .

Around 22.15 the home help, Irene Riggs, came back to the Villa Madeira after visiting her parents. She heard a strange, heavy breathing coming from somewhere in the house, but after a brief investigation thought no more of it. Her employer was not in his bedroom; no doubt he had dozed off downstairs. Upstairs, she met Stoner on the landing. He was wearing pyjamas and said he was checking to see that the lights were out. Irene Riggs then went to bed, and was briefly joined in her room by Mrs Rattenbury who often dropped in last thing at night to chat about the day's events. Alma seemed in good spirits, and was looking forward to the proposed trip to Bridport.

Alma then left, and Irene Riggs was just dozing off when she heard someone rushing downstairs. Alma's voice shrieked, 'Irene!' and the servant followed quickly down to the drawing room. The lights were on, and there in his chair sat her employer, his head a wreck of blood. Mrs Rattenbury was desperately trying to bring him round, cramming his false teeth into his mouth so that he could speak to them. Her first words to Irene were 'Someone has hurt Ratz! Telephone the doctor!'

In the panic which followed, Alma started drinking whisky continuously. The pair tried to bathe and bandage the victim. Mrs Rattenbury was specially worried that her little son John would come down and be frightened by the blood. The doctor arrived at 23.15 and a surgeon was called for. Later, an ambulance arrived at the Villa, but the victim was to die in the operating theatre without ever regaining consciousness.

By the time the police arrived at 02.00 Alma had consumed a lot of whisky. She was chattering, now, in hysterical fashion: she played records and danced and even tried to kiss a policeman. Out of the wild staccato of her utterances, several key phrases were recorded: 'I know who did it! I did it with a mallet! It is hidden . . . Ratz has lived too long. No, my lover did it. I will give you £10. No, I won't bribe you.'

Informed at about 03.30 that her husband's condition was critical, she said: 'I will tell you in the morning where the mallet is. I shall make a better job of it next time. I made a proper muddle of it. I thought I was strong enough.'

The doctor gave her an injection of morphia and put her to bed. She came round at one point and said: 'I know who did it – his son . . . but he is not here.' Lastly, when she appeared much calmer, she made a written statement:

About 9 p.m. on Sunday, 24th March 1935, I was playing cards with my husband when he dared me to kill him, as he wanted to die. I picked up the mallet. He then said: 'You have not guts enough to do it.' I then hit him with the mallet. I hid the mallet outside the house. I would have shot him if I'd had a gun.

When Mrs Rattenbury was being escorted from the house the next morning, she was met by Stoner who was heard to say: 'You have got yourself into this mess by talking too much.'

Stoner himself had been questioned by police during the night and claimed that the first he knew of the murder was when he heard Mrs Rattenbury shouting for help from the drawing room. Three days later, however, he made a confession: 'Do you know Mrs Rattenbury had nothing to do with the affair? When I did the job I believed he was asleep. I hit him, and then came upstairs and told Mrs Rattenbury. She rushed down then . . .'

What were people to believe? Each suspect had confessed to the murder, each claiming to be the sole person responsible. Which of them did it? Or had they collaborated in the assault and were now trying to shield each other?

The case was picked up by the national press which made the most of its sensational aspects. BOY CHAUFFEUR'S ORDEAL – STONER TOOK COCAINE – VORTEX OF ILLICIT LOVE – PYJAMAS AT 60/- A PAIR! screamed the headlines. And at the outset popular opinion was set firmly against Mrs Rattenbury. Alma was more than twice her lover's age, and seen both as adulteress and seducer. Stoner had been a perfectly normal, decent boy before he fell into her clutches. Perhaps the youth was only behaving chivalrously in confessing belatedly to his own guilt.

The trial was held at the Old Bailey, and the two accused were to be tried individually, but in the same court. This created problems in itself, since statements made in one case could not necessarily be used as evidence in the other. Further confusion was caused by the fact that both Mrs Rattenbury and her lover ended up by pleading not guilty. But for the public, the ultimate puzzle was provided by the fact that Stoner never entered the witness box. This could be interpreted in one of two ways. Either his counsel considered that his appearance would damage his own case or the boy was nobly refusing to say anything in the box which might incriminate Mrs Rattenbury.

It was, in fact, a trial of either/ors. But one certainty did emerge. The police had found the murder weapon, with blood and hairs on it, hidden behind a trellis in the garden. It was Stoner who had obtained the mallet – he had borrowed it from the home of his grandparents at 20.00 on the fateful evening.

Unlike Stoner, Alma did enter the witness box, and she made an impressive figure. She spoke in a low, clear voice which gave every appearance of truthfulness. Moreover, she was perfectly frank about her adultery.

She said that shortly after she phoned Mr Jenks to arrange the Bridport trip, Stoner had approached her in a jealous rage and cornered her in the dining room. He was emphatic that she should not go to Bridport with her husband. He threatened to kill her if she did. He claimed to have seen her making love to her husband that very afternoon in her bedroom.

Alma denied his claim, and tried to soothe all his fears about Bridport. She thought she had succeeded in calming her lover, but he left the house not long afterwards. The timing implied that it was about then that Stoner went off to fetch the mallet.

That night, having said goodnight to her husband and had her chat with Irene, Alma retired to her bedroom. Stoner joined her soon afterwards in his pyjamas, looking 'a little queer'. She asked what the matter was, and after much prompting he explained. 'He told me that I was not going to Bridport the next day as he had hurt Ratz. It did not penetrate my head what he did say to me at all until I heard Ratz groan, and then my brain became alive and I jumped out of bed . . .'

Downstairs with Irene she tried to revive her wounded husband. She also started drinking whisky 'to block out the picture'. The last thing she remembered was putting a white towel round her husband's head, and the episode with the false teeth. She had trodden on them with her bare feet. They had made her hysterical.

All that followed was a blank to her. The records, the dancing, the babbling, the bribe and the flirting with policemen – all were erased from her mind. She only 'came to' about midday the following morning.

Mrs Rattenbury's statements coincided closely with Irene's. In truth, there was precious little evidence against her apart from her own hysterical and contradictory confessions. Her temporary amnesia was curious, true. But it was not hard to see how the shock of the discovery, the whisky and the morphia might have combined to 'blank her mind'.

As the trial progressed, things pointed more and more to the guilt of the jealous young chauffeur. In fact, his defence counsel was reduced to trying to limit the damage by elaborating on his cocaine addiction. This, it was implied (but never stated) might account for an unreasoned attack for which a verdict of manslaughter might be appropriate. Unfortunately for the youth who stood silent in the dock, serious doubts were raised as to whether he even knew what cocaine looked like. Interviewed by a medical officer at Brixton, Stoner had been asked to describe the drug's appearance. He replied that it was brown with black flecks in it. Cocaine, of course, is a white powder.

The jury took little more than an hour to consider their verdict. They found Alma Victoria Rattenbury not guilty; and they found George Percy Stoner guilty.

Mrs Rattenbury faltered forward, calling weakly 'Oh . . . oh, no,' and was ushered hurriedly from the dock. Stoner was left standing manfully before the judge, a lone figure bravely containing his emotion. The black cloth was brought out. Asked if he had anything to say before sentence was passed, Stoner answered 'Nothing at all, sir.' They were the only words he spoke during the trial.

Often, the acquittal of a woman on a hanging offence has been greeted with cheers by the crowd. But they booed Mrs Rattenbury as she was hurried away in a taxi. Cruel words had been spoken about her in court; the judge himself had severely censured her conduct. Freedom would be no easy burden to bear. Above all, there was her young lover, waiting in the death cell – how could she endure the day when the trap door would be sprung?

On Tuesday 4 June, three days after her acquittal, Alma Rattenbury took a train on the London–Bournemouth line. But she did not reach the Villa Madeira. Instead, she alighted at Christchurch and wandered the backwaters of the River Avon. By a railway bridge (from which Stoner had once felt the impulse to hurl himself to his death), Mrs Rattenbury sat down in the grass and pencilled a few notes on the backs of envelopes taken from her handbag. 'One must be bold to do a thing like this. It is beautiful here, and I am alone. Thank God for peace at last . . .'

A farmworker nearby saw her walk into the lily-strewn water, a blade glinting in her hand. She gazed fixedly as she walked. He rushed towards her, but when he got there it was too late.

At the post mortem it was found that she had plunged the knife no fewer than six times into her chest. Three wounds had pierced her heart, one of them so severe that she must have worked the blade backwards and forwards before she withdrew it. Alma Rattenbury was dead before the water claimed her and carried her drifting from the bank.

Relief From Tension
You should not expect great depths of cunning from the passionate criminal. When a 78-year-old Florida man discovered that his wife was having an affair he resorted to violence. One day, while the woman was in bed with her paramour, the irate husband lobbed a petrol bomb through the window. Then he fled the scene.

It did not take the police long to nail their suspect. The unfortunate husband suffered acutely from constipation. The bottle he hurled had originally contained a well-known brand of prune juice.

THE WORLD'S GREATEST CRIMES OF PASSION

George Stoner, at the death cell in Pentonville, collapsed sobbing when he heard the news. A petition for his reprieve was already being gathered, to which thousands put their names. And four days after Alma's death, his lawyers lodged a formal appeal.

For the first time, Stoner submitted his own version of the events. He was entirely innocent of any part in the murder, he said. He had fetched the mallet for perfectly ordinary reasons and left it in the coal shed. When he made his way into Mrs Rattenbury's room that night, she appeared terrified. When a groan was heard from the drawing room, she leapt out of bed and rushed downstairs . . .

This was a remarkable twist to the tale. Was Mrs Rattenbury guilty after all? In the event, the judges decided that there was no case for an appeal, nor would they accept Stoner's new statement. It appeared no more than a cynical strategy to start making claims now that he would not make while his mistress was alive.

Stoner did not, however, hang. On the day after the appeal was turned down the Home Secretary granted a reprieve, and his death sentence was commuted to penal servitude for life.

Does an element of mystery still linger about the affair? If Stoner was guilty, what was it about the trip to Bridport that provoked his murderous wrath? An exhaustive study of the case (*Tragedy in Three Voices*, 1980) points to a piece of information which only came to light over forty years after the events. A friend of Alma's stated in a 1978 interview that she had asked Mrs Rattenbury in Holloway what had made Stoner so unusually angry. Alma replied that the chauffeur had overheard her conversation with her husband about the proposed business trip. 'Ratz', it appeared, had suggested to her that she use her charm on the Bridport man so that financial arrangements for the flats would go through smoothly. She might even have an affair with him if necessary.

This, by implication, was too much for the jealous lover. He could tolerate Alma's affectionate companionship with her elderly husband. But to countenance his beloved being used in this way was quite impossible.

It is a theory which fits the known facts. Stoner has commonly been represented in crime writing rather as Mrs Rattenbury's counsel portrayed him – as a youth whose love turned him into a 'Frankenstein's monster' with passions his mistress could not control. But that view misses the essential decency of the boy which everyone noted at the time. It was his decency which was outraged by the Bridport proposal, as much as his jealousy was aroused.

George Percy Stoner served only seven years in penal servitude. Released with good conduct during World War Two, he took part in the D-Day landings and after the war settled down to a respectable married life. Alma was buried at a Bournemouth cemetary in June 1935. Her shroud, wreaths and draperies were in pink, her favourite colour; she always had a horror of white.

The Kenya Scandal

It was January 1941. The Blitz had been raging over London for some six months, and in the sands of North Africa the see-saw struggle for Italy's desert colonies had begun. Kenya was then a British territory, and a mustering point for Allied forces planning the push on Mussolini's Ethiopia. At Nairobi, the Military Secretary was Josslyn Hay, Earl of Erroll and hereditary High Constable of Scotland.

During his brief career as an administrator, the 39-year-old Hay proved brilliant at his job. And his achievements came as something of a surprise to the settler community. For the Earl was chiefly notorious as a member of the Happy Valley Set, a permissive and pleasure-seeking section of the local white aristocracy.

Its centre was the Wanjohi river, cutting a declivity among the beautiful White Highlands of Kenya. One bastion of luxury was the exclusive Muthaiga Country Club, laid out with ballroom, golf course, squash courts and croquet lawns like something plucked from the landscape of the Home Counties. Cocaine circulated among the elite, and alcohol was consumed in great quantities: pink gins, sundowners, champagne and whiskey among the favourite tipples. By night, a mood of drunken licentiousness prevailed, and the denizens played roaring hooligan games.

Another centre of the Set was a large mansion called Clouds, the home of Lady Idina Gordon. The weekend house parties held there were notorious for their shameless excesses. Wives and partners were regularly swapped in the guest bedrooms. Josslyn Hay had flourished in this setting. He had been Lady Idina's third husband, and a predator in the jungle of luxury.

Dismissed from Eton and named as a 'very bad blackguard' by the judge in an English divorce court, Hay was a specialist in seduction. For quarry he preferred the wives and girlfriends of his aristocratic companions; his motto was 'to hell with husbands'. And when, in the early hours of 24 January 1941, he was found shot through the head on the floor of his Buick, no-one dwelled long on the possibility of a political murder. Predictably, the prime suspect was a husband: specifically, 57-year-old Sir Henry 'Jock' Delves Broughton.

The trial caused a sensation at the time. It was the scandal of Africa and followed with relish throughout the English-speaking world. The case came, no doubt, as a relief for a public weary with stories of bombings and evacuations. But it also provoked intense outrage, exposing an extravagant and dissolute way of life lived outside the cauldron of the war. The case continued to fascinate long after the fighting was over, and the question 'Who Killed Lord Erroll?' provided one of the world's classic unsolved mysteries.

Sir Henry Delves Broughton was a devotee of horse-racing and a member of a great English landowning family. In November 1940, he had married the glamorous Diana Caldwell, a blue-eyed ash-blonde who was young enough to be his daughter. Sir Henry was recently divorced from his first wife, and acknowledged the difficulties his new marriage might face by entering an extraordinary contract with Diana. Six weeks before the wedding, he agreed with her that if she fell for a younger man and wanted a divorce he would not stand in her way. Moreover, he agreed to provide her with £5,000 annually for at least seven years after a divorce.

The couple never shared a bedroom. And the contract implied no confidence in the durability of their relationship. But even Sir Henry cannot have anticipated how quickly his marriage was to come into jeopardy.

A week after the wedding, the Broughtons emigrated to Kenya. And on 30 November, at the Muthaiga Club, Diana met Lord Erroll for the first time. They fell for each other immediately. Diana later recalled that on the very first moment they found each other alone, Erroll said: 'Well, who's going to tell Jock? You or I?'

Erroll himself was free at the time: his first marriage to Idina Gordon had ended in divorce; his second wife, also a Countess, had died of drink and drugs in 1939. And he wasted no time in establishing his new liaison; but no-one told 'Jock' – not yet.

Soon, Broughton, Diana and Erroll were dining regularly together at the Club. The two men got on well together, for Broughton, like Erroll, was an Old Etonian. At his trial, the injured husband was to call his wife's lover 'one of the most amusing men I have ever met'. Broughton added that, 'if you can make a great friend in two months, then Joss Erroll I should describe as a great friend.'

It was not long before the passion shared by Diana and the Earl became conspicuous. At a party at the Club on 22 December, they could be seen dancing together locked in embrace. In the first week in January they shared a weekend alone together at the house of a discreet friend. And if Broughton had not guessed by now what was going on, there were alert eyes and ears all around. On Monday 6 January he found an anonymous note in the pigeon-hole at the Club. It read:

> You seemed like a cat on hot bricks at the club last night. What about
> the eternal triangle? What are you going to do about it?

What was he going to do about it? Broughton made light of the note with Diana, but the problem would not go away. At a party the following week, Broughton sat watching his wife dance with her lover. Lady Delamere, a mutual friend, said, 'Do you know that Joss is wildly in love with Diana?' By his own

Lord and Lady Erroll

admission, Broughton became rather distrait: 'It confirmed my worst suspicions.' He did not try to break up the liaison, but he did talk over the situation subsequently with Diana: 'I think you are going out rather too much with Joss.'

This meek reprimand was ignored; the affair continued and Broughton took to drinking more heavily than usual. Seeking advice from a friend, he was told that he should ask Erroll if he was really in love with Diana. 'If he says no, tell him to buzz off. If they are in love with each other, cut your losses. Pack your boxes and get off back to England.'

The pressure was mounting. Not long after this conversation, Broughton received a second anonymous note:

Do you know that your wife and Lord Erroll have been
staying alone at the Carberrys' house at Nyeri together?

On that same afternoon, 18th January, Diana broke the ice and said she was in love with Erroll. The Broughtons had been married barely two months.

Broughton tried to stall. He had been planning a 3-month trip to Ceylon and suggested that she should come with him to see how her feelings were affected. He also saw Erroll, proposing that Diana should accompany him on the Ceylon trip, and that Erroll might leave Kenya for a while.

Erroll, of course, was an old hand at dealing with injured husbands. He said he could not possibly go away – after all, 'there was a *war* on.'

The situation had reached an impasse. That night, Broughton went home alone while Diana and Erroll dined out with friends at the Muthaiga Club. She came back wearing a new set of pearls – a gift to her from her lover.

The following sequence of events had immense importance in the coming trial. The next day, Diana declared that she could not remain in her husband's house under the circumstances, and went off with a friend to stay at Erroll's. On 21 January, while she was away, Broughton reported a burglary to the police. He said that two revolvers, a cigarette case and a small sum of money had been stolen from his living room.

Also on the 21st, Broughton and Erroll both saw their lawyers about a divorce. On the surface at least, Sir Henry appeared ready to capitulate, for he wrote to a friend, 'They say they are in love with each other and mean to get married. It is a hopeless position and I'm going to cut my losses. I think I'll go to Ceylon. There's nothing for me to live in Kenya for.' He also received a third anonymous note:

There's no fool like an old fool. What are
you going to do about it?

The 23rd January was a fateful day for all of the parties concerned. The three principals in the drama lunched with a fourth friend, Mrs Carberry, at the Muthaiga Club. Erroll told a colleague, 'Jock could not have been nicer. He has agreed to go away. As a matter of fact, he has been so nice it smells bad.'

There was a celebration dinner at the Club that night. And there, Broughton astonished everyone by proposing a toast to the lovers: 'I wish them every happiness,' he said. 'and may their union be blessed with an heir. To Diana and Joss.'

Erroll took Diana dancing that night, having agreed to bring her back by 03.00. Broughton was driven home at about 02.00, apparently tired and somewhat drunk. June Carberry helped him upstairs, and they said goodnight before she retired to her room.

Erroll's Buick turned up some 15 minutes later. There was laughter in the hall, the car door was heard slamming, and Diana came upstairs.

Around 03.00 that morning, two African labourers saw the Buick off the main Nairobi-Ngong road. It had travelled only $2\frac{1}{2}$ miles from the Broughtons' home, and though its lights were blazing the vehicle had plunged steeply into a pit off the wrong side of the road, 150 yards ahead of an intersection. Crouching under the dashboard was the body of Lord Erroll. His hands were clasped in front of his head. When police examined the corpse, it was found that he had been shot thr ugh the head at point-blank range with a .32 calibre revolver.

Much about the circumstances was perplexing. For example, the car had armslings which, it was known, had been in place on the day before the murder. These had been removed – wrenched off or unscrewed – and lay on the floor of the car. The position of the fatal wound suggested that Erroll had been shot either by someone sitting on the seat beside him, or through the open window from the running board. Had the murderer flagged Erroll down on the road, or been in the car with him all the time? And how did the body of a full-grown man get to be crowded down into the footwell? Had it slipped there as the car lurched – or been crammed under the wheel on purpose?

Precisely *how* the murder was accomplished remains a complete mystery to this day. But it did not take the police long to establish a prime suspect. Enquiries quickly revealed that Sir Henry had both the motive and the opportunity. The fact of murder was hushed up for 24 hours, and the Broughtons were first led to believe that Erroll had broken his neck in a motor accident. When the police arrived to take statements that morning, Diana was hysterical and not pressed for questioning. Broughton's immediate reaction was to ask 'Is he all right? Is he all right?'

Before noon, Broughton drove into Nairobi. He said that Diana wanted a handkerchief placed on the dead man's body: 'My wife was very much in love with Lord Erroll,' he explained. He seemed very nervous as he made the request, and was not permitted to enter the mortuary. A policeman, however, took the handkerchief and performed the office.

Returning home just after midday, Broughton immediately made a big bonfire in the rubbish pit in the grounds. He ordered his head boy to bring petrol for the blaze; it was a curious act under the circumstances. Broughton explained it at the trial by saying that he just liked making bonfires, and always had, ever since childhood. The charred remains of a golf stocking were all that were retrieved from the site. That stocking, however, was bloodstained – with the blood of his victim? The police began to assemble their case.

Erroll's funeral was held on 25 January. Broughton arrived late, and dropped a letter from his wife onto the coffin of the Earl. Ever watchful, the police had the scrap of paper exhumed. It turned out to be a simple love-note. On one side, Diana had written 'I love you desperately', and on the back Erroll had replied, 'and I love you forever.'

When the fact of murder was publicly announced, Diana loudly accused her husband of the crime. Broughton made no reply. But on 10 March, when her husband was arrested, her mood softened. It was Diana who went to Johannesburg to hire the most brilliant advocate in Africa. His name was H.H. Morris, K.C., and he specialised in winning difficult murder cases.

The prosecution had its motive. And it had much more besides. There was the business of the burglary, for example. One of the guns 'stolen' on that occasion had been a .32 calibre weapon. Broughton had done some target practice with it when he first arrived in Kenya. And, searching the informal practice ground, the police found four .32 calibre bullets which, it was alleged, exactly matched two discovered at the scene of the crime. The murder weapon, in other words, was Broughton's own gun – and the 'burglary' had been a pure invention.

To confirm its thesis, the prosecution went on to point out that all six bullets had been fired with an old-fashioned 'black powder' propellant. This had been unobtainable in Kenya for more than 25 years. A ballistics expert testified that the chances of two people using black powder bullets were remote in the extreme.

Could the elderly Broughton have made it to and from the murder point in the time available to him? According to Mrs Carberry, he knocked on the door of her room at about 03.30 to ask 'if she needed anything'. This, according to the prosecution, was 'a most peculiar thing to do.' But it made sense as an attempt to establish an alibi. Imagine the scenario: Broughton slips out of the house when the couple return. Then he furtively enters the car – or runs to the road junction – and murders his rival out of earshot. Hastening back to his home, he knocks on Mrs Carberry's door solely to give the impression that he never left the house.

There was the mysterious bonfire, and the bloodstained golf stocking – all suggesting a carefully premeditated plot and a subsequent cover-up. Presumably, the planning began with the fake theft of the revolvers and included the magnanimous champagne toast at the Club. Of course, it implied a considerable deviousness on the part of the murderer. But this was an era when Agatha Christie was all the rage: the case against Sir Henry looked formidable.

Sir Henry and Lady Broughton and Colonel Sam Ashton leaving for Africa

Yet from the outset of the trial, the defence counsel, Harry Morris, had made it known that he had something up his sleeve. It was something simple, he said, 'so simple that I almost mistrust it.' But he would not divulge what that secret was – not even to the defendant.

The bombshell burst during cross-examination on the ballistics evidence. The experts had testified that all six bullets came from the same .32 calibre revolver, with five grooves and a right-hand twist. Morris asked innocently whether these were features of Colt revolvers. No, came the reply, all Colts had six grooves and a twist to the left. So the murder bullets could not have been fired from a Colt? The expert agreed that they could not.

Now Morris played his trump. He let it be known that Broughton's two stolen revolvers were registered as Colts – the firearms certificates confirmed it. Erroll, then, could not have been shot with one of the stolen guns!

For a *coup de grâce*, Morris pointed out that the murder weapon had not been recovered. And its barrel was needed to positively identify the practice bullets Broughton had fired with the two found at the scene of the crime. He pressed the ballistics expert: 'The claim that all six bullets were fired from the same weapon cannot be proved. Is that not so, Mr Harwich?'

'It is.'

Suddenly, the prosecution's case against Sir Henry began to look terribly shaky. The 'black powder' issue became practically irrelevant. And with nothing to connect Broughton in any way with the murder weapon, what did remain as hard evidence against him? The motive? Yet even before his marriage Sir Henry had indicated by the contract that he was the least possessive of husbands. He made a dignified and impressive figure in the witness box: a little forgetful it is true on some points of detail (he did not recall knocking on Mrs Carberry's door, for example). But he was quite candid about being cuckolded. Once, for example, he had invited Erroll to stay the night in full knowledge of his wife's adultery: 'She could ask whom she liked. I should not have tried to stop her in any event. I see no point in it. We met every day at the club and I cannot see it makes any difference if a man comes to stay the night. It would be extremely bad strategy. In my experience of life, if you try and stop a woman doing anything she wants to do it all the more. With a young wife the only thing to do is keep her amused.'

As to the famous toast to Diana and Joss, was that sincere on his part? 'Certainly it was. The whole party was very happy and everybody on their top form. I was resigned to losing my wife and I cut my loss.'

Broughton was masterful during his three days of cross-examination. He came across as a bluff old racing man who had known when he was beaten. Could the deviousness implied by the prosecution really be imputed to him? Harry Morris did not think so, for he returned to Johannesburg without even bothering to wait for the verdict. When it came, on 1 July 1941, Broughton was found not guilty, and he walked from the court a free man.

Did he really do it? And if not, who did? Rumour was rife in Kenya's white community. There were other injured husbands to consider; there was talk of hired native assassins. Then there were the women of the Happy Valley Set: those who plumped for a female killer tended to opt for the chic, exquisite and faintly mad Alice de Janzé, a one-time lover of Erroll's. She was no stranger to firearms – she had once shot herself and an earlier lover on the platform of the Paris Gare du Nord; both had survived and she was acquitted of attempted murder on the grounds of *crime passionnel*. In Kenya at the time of the Erroll murder, Alice visited the Earl in the mortuary where she placed the branch of a tree on his body. According to a friend, she also kissed his body saying 'Now you're mine forever.' Later that year she committed suicide in a flower-filled room asking (in true Happy Valley style) that a cocktail party be held over her grave.

In truth, however, she was just one among Kenya's élite whose name was linked with the affair. There were so many loose ends: who, for example, had written the anonymous letters to Broughton?

The Happy Valley Set never survived the scandal, and Broughton never recovered from the stigma of the trial. He did take Diana on the long-projected trip to Ceylon, but there suffered a back injury which partially paralysed him. On 5 December 1942, he died in Liverpool having taken massive overdoses of Medinal. He left two suicide notes referring to the strain of the trial and the pain of his recent injury. He did not, in the text, declare himself guilty of murder, however.

Forty years after the events described, the case continued to fascinate and torment. Through painstaking research and interviews with survivors, reporter James Fox produced a brilliant study of the Erroll affair (*White Mischief*, Jonathan Cape, 1982). The book arrives at a firmly implied conclusion about the murderer's identity. It would be invidious to betray the last pages of this account of a real-life Whodunit. But it is fair to comment that Sir Henry Delves Broughton's background included some shady episodes. Suspicions of devious insurance fraud and blackmail attach to the memory of the reasonable old cove who walked free from the Kenya courtroom.

Saved by a Judge's Blunder

It probably qualifies as the World's Easiest Murder Mystery. Everyone knew who killed Rose Pender in the early hours of 21 August 1911. The suspect's name, his motive and his murder weapon were clearly established at the trial. But because of a judicial blunder, the murderer walked free from the Court of Criminal Appeal. Officially, the case remains open.

It was a seedy affair, peopled with wretched and depraved characters from the London underworld. Thieves, pimps and prostitutes filed into the witness box to give evidence at the Old Bailey. At the outset, no-one could have imagined that the case would become an historic one, marking a watershed in British legal history.

THE WORLD'S GREATEST CRIMES OF PASSION

Charles Ellsome, who described himself as a labourer, was brought to the dock in September 1911, for the murder of Rose Pender, his mistress. She was a prostitute, 19 years of age, and Ellsome had lived on her immoral earnings. And when she eventually left him for an Italian boy, Ellsome publicly threatened vengeance.

A few days before the fateful night, Ellsome borrowed a shilling from a friend and with it bought a long-bladed chef's knife. He told the same friend, 'I am going to do that Italian in for taking Rosie away.' In the small hours of the 21st, a man on his way to work in Clerkenwell heard a girl's voice crying, 'Don't, Charles! Don't!' Later, a milkman found Rose's dead body in the street, bloodstained with multiple stab wounds.

Police enquiries quickly revealed Ellsome to be the prime suspect. Prostitute friends of the victim confirmed that for some time her ex-lover had been threatening to do Rosie in. To one witness he had even confided, 'A fortune-teller told me the gallows were in my cards, and that she was the girl I should swing for.'

On the 22nd Ellsome was tracked down and arrested. He gave his name as 'Brown' to police, but he said, 'It's me you want.' And a thief named Fletcher supplied damning evidence by describing how, shortly after the body was found, Ellsome had come to his house in a breathless condition and confessed the murder to him.

The case came to trial at Court No. 1 at the Old Bailey. The curious procession of miscreants was brought into the box to give evidence. And Mr Justice Avory, a usually meticulous judge, presided over all. In fairness to him it should be said that he had endured a very heavy week. The court agenda was crowded, and only that morning he had summed up at the end of a wife-murderer's trial. The Ellsome case came up after lunch – it lasted only for one extended afternoon session.

Formidable evidence was heard against the accused, the chief prosecution witness being the thief, Jack Fletcher. He lived with two ladies of the streets, and testified that when Ellsome arrived at his house on the murder night, he announced, 'I have killed her stone dead.'

Fletcher asked who he had killed, and Ellsome replied, 'Rosie, my missus. I killed her stone dead, Jack. She drove me to it.'

Ellsome had then produced the knife and showed it to his friend. He said he had met the girl by chance in the street and explained exactly how things happened: 'I asked her to come back to me, but she said she liked her Italian boy best. Then I lost my temper, pulled out the knife, showed it to her and said, 'I'll kill you first.' She said, 'Here you are then; I don't care' – and bared her breasts. I plunged the knife in. She cried, 'Don't, Charlie, don't,' and I knew I had done the damage, so I stabbed her eight or nine times afterwards.'

Fletcher's two women had been in the house at the time, and they corroborated his account. When interviewed by the police, Fletcher himself had made further statements, filling in additional details but in no way departing from his original story.

For the defence, it was a hopeless case. The accused had no alibi, and the best that the defence counsel could do was to try and cast aspersions on the character of the various witnesses. Fletcher, in particular, came in for a grilling, and emerged as a rather flash character. It was learned that he carried a police whistle in his pocket (it came in handy when danger threatened in some of his low-life locales). And it was clear that he knew the courtroom ropes. At one point the defence counsel asked:

'You are very nicely dressed; where did you get the clothes from?'

'Singing outside theatres.'

'May I suggest that it was by thieving?'

'This is a case of murder, and not felony, and I refuse to answer.'

'I must ask you, however?'

'Well, then, I thieve for my living and am proud of it.'

The judge began his summing up in the most impeccable way. He started by explaining that if the character of a witness was questionable, then corroboration was of vital importance. Then he made his blunder. He suggested that there was no discrepancy between the thief's first statement to police and his evidence in the witness box.

This was perfectly true. But the first statement (which had been produced at the police court trial) had never been put in evidence at the Old Bailey. Technically, it was quite improper to direct the jury that Fletcher's evidence was corroborated by his first statement. The jury had not seen the document in question.

Did the jury even notice the slip? It took them less than an hour to bring in their verdict of guilty. Asked if the prisoner had anything to say, Ellsome replied:

'No, sir. I have only one Judge.'

Mr Justice Avory brought out the black cap, and Ellsome was sentenced to

---

Peculiar Passion

New York – A man who allegedly broke into a house twice to tickle the feet of two sleeping sisters has been arrested and charged with burglary. 'He just likes women's feet,' a detective said. 'Some people like other parts of the female body, and he just likes feet.'

The Times

death. But he never went to the gallows. His defence counsel, A.S. Carr, was quick to pounce on the judge's error. It had come like a gift from the gods, and while his client awaited the end in the condemned cell, Carr took the case to the Court of Criminal Appeal.

This was a newly founded institution, set up in 1907 after considerable public pressure. Behind it lay a humane concern for victims of miscarried justice. The court might allow an appeal if it considered that the verdict of a jury was unreasonable, or could not be supported by the evidence – or that the judgement should be set aside on a point of law.

Until the Ellsome affair, no appeal in a murder case had succeeded. But on the issue in hand, Mr Justice Darling ruled that there was really no option. Indisputably, the Old Bailey judge had misdirected the jury by introducing a statement which was not in evidence. Darling regretted that the Court had no power to order a new trial. He declared that the Court could not express any view as to whether Ellsome was guilty or not. But he quashed the conviction – and Ellsome walked out of the Appeal Court a free man.

There was a tremendous irony in the ruling. The Court had been established to protect the innocent; a guilty man was acquitted on the first successful appeal. In the event, the Court survived as a valued institution – but it was 20 years before another convicted murderer was to make a successful appeal.

Death in the House of Cards

There are 52 cards in a deck. And when the famous bridge and whist expert Joseph Elwell was found murdered at his New York home, the police quickly came up with a list of suspects. Elwell had so many mistresses that he had to keep records of their names and addresses. In his desk was found a card index containing a host of entries, with pet names and telephone numbers. In all, 53 women were recorded. You could call it a full deck of suspects – and perhaps the extra card was the maverick Joker that brought his outstanding career to an end.

Joseph B. Elwell had started his working life as a Brooklyn hardware salesman. But from adolescence onwards, he had excelled at card-playing. Bridge and whist were his favoured games, and in his early twenties he was already winning big stakes at the fashionable New York gambling clubs. It was not long before he gave up selling hardware to teach bridge to wealthy socialites. And he also wrote two authoritative books about the game. *Elwell on Bridge* and *Elwell's Advanced Bridge* were classics in their day.

He married in 1904, and had a son the following year. With his winnings, his royalties and his tutoring fees he was soon able to set up home in Manhattan. By 1916, when Elwell separated from his wife, he was already a wealthy man. For his estranged spouse he set aside $2,400 a year, as well as paying all his son's expenses. The sums involved were trifling. From his book sales alone, Elwell was said to be receiving some $10,000 per annum, and this was a fraction of his total income.

Bridge is more of a science than a game – it is no diversion for reckless gamblers. Elwell invested his earnings wisely. Apart from following up financial tips offered by his wealthy pupils, he diversified into horse-racing. Not by betting, of course: Elwell set up the Beach Racing Stable, supplied from a Kentucky stud farm where he owned some two score thoroughbreds. His partner in the enterprise was William H. Pendleton, a prominent man of the turf.

By 1920, the year of his murder, Elwell had a yacht, an art collection and three separate cottage retreats. In New York, he lived in a three-storey house in West Seventieth Street. Apart from his own bachelor suite, there was a special guest boudoir for female visitors. This was luxuriously furnished, and the ladies came in exotic succession: wealthy wives, fashionable divorcées, glamorous show girls, titled women and many others. His appetite is attested by his card index file – and by other material found in the house. The police discovered dozens of love letters, photographs, and even a kind of pension list recording sums paid monthly to discarded mistresses.

On the evening of 10 June 1920, Elwell went to dine at the Ritz-Carlton Club. His female escort on that occasion was Viola Kraus, a woman divorced that very day. Her sister, Mrs Lewisohn, was present with her husband Walter Lewisohn, a businessman connected with the show world.

By a curious coincidence, the foursome ran into Viola's ex-husband at the Club. His name was Victor von Schlegell, and he was dining with a young lady singer. There seems to have been no rancour between the recently divorced couple, and all laughed heartily over the encounter. They were to laugh again later that night. For Elwell's party went on to the New Amsterdam Theatre where *Midnight Frolics* was playing. Who should be sitting at an almost adjacent table but von Schlegell and his young singer? Victor quipped at the time, 'I can't keep away from Vi even if the judge said today that we needn't be together again.'

The evening's entertainment ended at 02.00. The Lewisohns offered Elwell a lift home in their taxi, but the card-player claimed it was too crowded. He had also had a slight tiff with Viola, which may account for the refusal. Instead, he stopped a cab for himself and was driven home alone. The driver was to testify that, having received a tip from him, he saw Elwell enter the door of his house at 02.30.

Elwell employed three people as domestic staff: a valet, a chauffeur and a housekeeper. But none of them lived on the premises. To find out what happened behind the locked doors that night, the police were to consult telephone company records.

Shortly after his arrival, Viola phoned him, perhaps to patch up the quarrel. As a card-player, Elwell was something of a night-hawk and does not seem to have slept much afterwards. At 04.39 he rang his racing colleague, Pendleton, but received no reply and put the phone down after 5 minutes. At 06.09, Elwell telephoned a Long Island number. Whom he called is still not known to this day.

Dawn light broke over New York and the milkman deposited his bottles at the house. At 07.10 the postman delivered the mail. Elwell was still alive at that time. For when the housekeeper arrived at 08.10, she found her employer sitting in his pajamas in a living-room armchair. The morning mail was on the floor before him, an open letter was in his lap. And exactly between his eyes was the hole left by a .45 calibre bullet.

Blood from the wound stained carpet and pajamas, spattering the wall behind the chair. Elwell was still breathing, though unconscious – he died in hospital some two hours later.

The case was perfectly baffling. The two side-doors into the house were firmly locked, and the housekeeper had found the front door locked too. All the windows were fastened from the inside, except Elwell's own inaccessible window on the third floor. Murder by an intruding burglar appeared to be deeply improbable. There was no sign of a break-in, no sign of a struggle. Assorted items of jewellery as well as $400 in notes lay untouched about the house. Besides, what self-respecting burglar would still be on the premises so late into the morning?

The front door lock had recently been changed. Only Elwell and the housekeeper, Mrs Larsen, possessed keys. Everything pointed to the conclusion that the victim himself had admitted someone into the house. And the circumstantial detail suggested that, if the murderer was a woman, he must have known her very intimately.

The bridge expert was a vain man. Aged 45, he customarily wore a plate of false teeth to fill the gaps in his smile. He was balding, too, and wore a toupé (he had 40 of them in all). When Elwell was found barefoot and dying in his pajamas, he was wearing neither wig nor denture. Those accessories were found neatly placed on the dresser. It was unlikely he would have invited a lady in, unless on sufficiently intimate terms to have seen him like that before.

Elwell was shot between 07.10 (when the post arrived) and 08.10 (when the housekeeper found him dying). Medical experts further determined that he had been hit at least 45 minutes before Mrs Larsen arrived. That meant that the shot had been fired between 07.10 and 07.25. But of course, it was possible that the killer had been with Elwell in the house for hours beforehand – especially if the murderer was a bedroom companion.

Had he entertained a woman that night? It seemed unlikely, for his own bed appeared to have been only lightly lain upon. The cover was turned back and the pillow slightly dented, as if he had relaxed there on the sultry June night. The pillow beside his was undented; and in the guest boudoir, the bed was perfectly made. A pink silk kimono was, however, found hanging in the wardrobe. Given the number of his mistresses, the possibility of a female killer could not be entirely discounted.

Of course, the bewildering variety of his bedmates all had their attendant lovers, husbands or relations. Ballistic evidence did tend to suggest a male murderer. Elwell had been shot with a heavy .45 calibre army automatic pistol; hardly an obvious choice of weapon for a woman. The U.S. service cartridge was found, and the shot was a clean one fired from some 3–4 feet. Close range, certainly – but not point blank. The gun, moreover, seemed to have been fired from the hip, or from a crouching position. The bullet had followed an upward trajectory, entering the forehead, exiting an inch higher at the back and going on upwards to smash against the wall. By a macabre chance it had then ricocheted back to land quite neatly on the side table right by the victim's elbow.

The murderer had disturbed nothing, left no fingerprint. The only remaining clue was one cigarette stub (of a brand other than Elwell used) found on the living-room mantlepiece.

Hazily, the picture suggested a brief visit, probably made after the mail arrived. Elwell admitted the murderer and was so unconcerned in his or her presence that he went on riffling through his letters. He had permitted the gun to be drawn and the murderer to approach within little more than a yard before firing.

It might, of course, have been a business associate. But Elwell had no special rivals: his racing-stable partner was among those questioned and he was fully exonerated. For the police, however, the bridge expert's love life opened up a Pandora's Box of possibilities. All 53 women named in the card index were investigated and closely questioned, along with others, men and women, discovered through the letters. Husbands, lovers and relations were also explored – everyone appeared to have an alibi. One by one the suspects were ticked off – the valet, the chauffeur, the housekeeper's husband, a Polish countess, an Egyptian princess . . . the list of possibilities appeared endless.

THE WORLD'S GREATEST CRIMES OF PASSION

Names that featured repeatedly in the press stories included three prominent suspects:

Mrs Elwell The estranged wife had learned some time before the murder that her husband had struck her out of his will. But she had a cast-iron alibi. Moreover, she stood to lose by Elwell's death, for her son's expenses and the $2,400 a year would be cut off.

Viola Kraus She had been with Elwell on the murder night, they had quarrelled and she had phoned him at his home. It was also established that she was the owner of the pink silk kimono in the boudoir. However, the Lewisohns testified that she was with them at their home overnight and through the murder period.

Victor von Schlegell Did Viola's husband, so recently divorced, still feel possessive about her? Victor had breakfasted with his young singer on the following morning, but went out early to pick up his car from a garage. He arrived there at 08.00, and might *just* have had time to kill Elwell before arriving at the garage. However, nothing indicates that he had any jealous feelings about Viola (he married his singer in due course).

No solution was ever found. But in the realm of pure speculation it is interesting to consider the enigma of 'Annie'.

One of the letters found in Elwell's desk had been sent by a 16-year-old Kentucky girl. She signed herself simply 'Annie' and complained to Elwell that she was going to get 'into trouble'. She begged him to 'do the right thing' by her.

Sidney Sutherland, a writer of the 1920s, toyed with the idea that her father, or brother, may have come to New York to persuade Elwell to 'do the right thing', and plugged him between the eyes when he refused. It is as plausible a theory as any: you can imagine Annie's seduction on one of Elwell's trips to the stud farm. You can picture the straight-shootin' Kentucky man with his old service pistol. He arrives by dawn light and puts his proposition fair and square to the rich northern city slicker. Toothless and balding in his expensive pajamas, Elwell brushes him off and returns petulantly to his armchair and his mail. One shot (it has to be from the hip) sees off the card player. The avenger nonchalantly stubs out his cigarette and goes back to Kentucky, never speaking of the episode again.

Plausible – but pure hypothesis. The fact is that the Elwell murder remains a complete and utter mystery; and every theory is as insubstantial as a house of cards.

'Are You Going to Sleep All Day?'

At 14.30 in the afternoon of Sunday 24 October 1943, the nanny at Patricia Lonergan's apartment knocked at the door of her mistress's bedroom. 'Young woman,' she cried, 'are you going to sleep all day?'

There was no reply. The heiress had returned from a late-night party in the small hours of the morning, and the nanny took the 18-month-old baby out. She did not return with the child until 7 in the evening when she tried the door again. It was still locked, and still there was no reply. Disturbed now by the ominous silence, the nanny sent for help. The door could not be broken down – it had to be removed bodily from its frame. And when the helpers finally attained the bedroom they discovered a grim tableau.

The nude body of the 22-year-old heiress was sprawled out across her wide bed, overlooked by its bronzed figures of Winged Victory. Blood had seeped from her head wounds through the sheets and blankets, down through the mattress and on to the floor where it formed a large dark stain. Mrs Patricia Burton Lonergan, heiress to a seven million dollar brewing fortune, would not be awakening that evening or ever again. She was dead: strangled and bludgeoned, police were to establish, by the pair of antique onyx-inlaid brass candlesticks that lay discarded on the floor.

The assailant had evidently fled via a second, automatically sprung door. It did not look like the work of a thief, for there was cash and jewellery in the suite as well as the victim's mink jacket neatly folded at the foot of the bed. But the struggle had been a violent one in which the heiress had scratched her attacker: traces of scraped skin were found under her manicured fingernails. In due course, the police were to establish that the time of death was about 09.00. Patricia Lonergan had been a corpse all day.

In the investigation which followed, police brought in her escort of the night before. He was Mario Gabelline, a 40-year-old Italian man-about-town. He stated that he had brought the heiress back to her apartment at 06.15 in the morning, but had left her in the lobby and returned immediately to his waiting cab. The taxi-driver was traced and confirmed his story. Gabelline was held on bail as a material witness, but he made an unlikely suspect.

More suspicion attached to Wayne Lonergan, 27-year-old former husband of the victim. He had been separated from the heiress only two months before the murder and had gone to live in Canada. Having no private means, he enlisted as a serviceman in the Royal Canadian Air Force. Though he lived in Toronto, it was discovered that Lonergan had been in New York on the weekend of the murder, staying in a friend's apartment.

Some curious facts were discovered about Wayne Lonergan's movements. On the Saturday evening he had gone to his ex-wife's apartment. He found that she was out, but was admitted by staff and played with his child for a while. That night he had taken an attractive blonde on a tour of New York night clubs before leaving her at her home at 03.00. Then (so it seemed) he retired to the friend's apartment where he wakened at about 10.30. He had called loudly for coffee and scrambled eggs, and phoned to make a lunch date with the blonde. When he turned up for the meal, he was not wearing his blue serviceman's uniform as he had done before. Instead, he was wearing a grey suit that ill-fitted his 6 ft 2 in frame. An explanation for his garb was discovered in the friend's apartment, in the form of a hastily written note:

> John: Thank you so much for the use of your flat. Due to a slight case of mistaken trust, I lost my uniform and so borrowed a jacket and trousers from you. I shall return these on my arrival in Toronto.
>
> > Yours,
> > Wayne.
>
> PS – I will call and tell you about it.

Another discovery was made at the apartment too: in the drawer of the owner's desk was the plate of scrambled eggs that he had ordered for his Sunday breakfast.

Apprehended in Toronto, Lonergan appeared not to know what fate had befallen his ex-wife. He explained the business of the missing uniform by saying that after taking the blonde home early on the fateful Sunday morning, he had gone for a short stroll and met a US soldier waiting for a bus. They fell into conversation and Lonergan offered to put him up. On waking, he discovered not only his uniform but also some money gone. The soldier's name, he said was Murray Worcester and he was stationed somewhere on the East Coast. As for the enigmatic scrambled eggs, he had ordered them for the dog that his friend kept in the apartment. When the dog failed to show up, Lonergan hid the eggs not wanting to appear wasteful.

When first approached in Toronto, Lonergan had scratch marks on his chin. He claimed that he had recently cut himself shaving. To detectives who regarded him as the prime suspect, there came baffling confirmation: not only the blonde, but other witnesses too had seen him during the course of the Sunday. They were emphatic in declaring that his chin at the time was unmarked.

Nor had Lonergan appeared in any way to be in an excitable state. In fact, prior to the lunch, he had gone round to his ex-wife's apartment taking with him a 3 ft toy elephant for his son. He arrived some time after eleven, and receiving no answer left the toy with the note: 'For Master Billy Lonergan.'

The case aroused intense interest in the press. Patricia Lonergan, the beautiful socialite, had been immensely rich, living on an annual income of $25,000. Lonergan, in contrast, had lived a chequered life and had been a tie salesman on Madison Avenue when first introduced to the heiress. The couple had eloped to marry in Las Vegas in July 1941, and when Patricia bore a child it seems that she wanted to settle down. Lonergan, though, had enjoyed the life of luxurious irresponsibility. Only two months before the murder, the couple had separated and Mrs Lonergan had cut him out of her will.

While the newspapers speculated about the murder and its motives, Lonergan was persuaded to return to New York where he faced a severe grilling by detectives. At one stage he was confronted with a tall thin man that he said he had never seen before in his life. The man was Mr Maurice Worcester, a former US soldier, traced through searches of army records. The police were to claim that Lonergan had simply plucked the man's name out of thin air in seeking to explain the theft of the missing uniform. It was purely by chance that a real Maurice Worcester existed – and hardly surprising that Lonergan failed to recognise him.

After 84 hours of questioning, Lonergan made a confession which was leaked to the press. He said that he had slipped out of his friend's apartment on the murder morning, and arrived at Patricia's apartment shortly before 09.00. She was in bed and they quarrelled over Lonergan's intention to have lunch with the blonde. In a jealous rage, Patricia shoved him from her, shouting, 'Stay out of here, don't ever come back. You will never see the baby again!'

This, in Lonergan's version, provoked his fatal assault. Afterwards, at his friend's apartment, he rang for breakfast but found that he could not eat and so hid the plate of scrambled eggs, not wanting to arouse suspicion. He packed his bloodstained uniform in a duffel bag and dropped it, weighted with a dumbell, into the East River.

As for the scratch marks missing from his chin at the lunch date, police found a simple explanation. A powder compact containing Max Factor Suntan No. 2 was discovered in the friend's apartment. It was contended that Lonergan had bought this at a drugstore shortly after fleeing the scene of the crime. Careful application of the heavy cream was all that was needed to camouflage evidence of the fight.

Wayne Lonergan was indicted for first degree murder, and after a mistrial in February 1944, was tried again in March. Effectively, through the leaked confession, the press had found him guilty already. But some irregularities emerged in the courtroom.

Lonergan pleaded not guilty. His defence contended that he had been offered the lower plea of second degree murder if he would confess. In fact, the confession was not signed or authenticated by him. It was never shown that Lonergan had visited the apartment at the time of the murder, nor that he had handled the onyx candlesticks. Above all, he had no motive for deliberately killing his ex-wife. He was not jealous of her Italian escort, nor did he stand to gain financially by her death. The prosecution's case left room for reasonable doubt: a panic-stricken intruder might have been responsible.

In the event, the jury was out for more than 9 hours, and returned with a verdict of guilty to murder in the second degree (murder without premeditation). On 17 April 1944, the prisoner was sentenced to 35 years to life imprisonment.

Wayne Lonergan served 22 years in Sing Sing, and was paroled in 1965.